D1297303

THE PRINCIPAL'S OFFICE

A Primer for Balanced Leadership

Jan Irons Harris

ROWMAN & LITTLEFIELD PUBLISHERS, INC.

Lanham • New York • Toronto • Plymouth, UK

ROWMAN & LITTLEFIELD PUBLISHERS, INC.

Published in the United States of America
by Rowman & Littlefield Education
A Division of Rowman & Littlefield Publishers, Inc.
A wholly owned subsidiary of The Rowman & Littlefield Publishing Group, Inc.
4501 Forbes Boulevard, Suite 200, Lanham, Maryland 20706
www.rowmaneducation.com

Estover Road
Plymouth PL6 7PY
United Kingdom

British Library Cataloguing in Publication Information Available

Library of Congress Cataloging-in-Publication Data

Harris, Jan Irons, 1960–
    The principal's office : a primer for balanced leadership / Jan Irons Harris.
        p. cm.
    Includes bibliographical references.
    ISBN-13: 978-1-57886-838-4 (cloth : alk. paper)
    ISBN-10: 1-57886-838-6 (cloth : alk. paper)
    ISBN-13: 978-1-57886-839-1 (pbk. : alk. paper)
    ISBN-10: 1-57886-839-4 (pbk. : alk. paper)
    eISBN-13: 978-1-57886-899-5
    eISBN-10: 1-57886-899-8
1. School principals. I. Title.
    LB2831.9.H365 2008
    371.2'012—dc22   2008013950

Manufactured in the United States of America.

This book is dedicated to my loving parents, Bobby and Sara Irons, who taught me by example what it means to live a balanced life. Mother and Daddy, thank you for helping me to achieve my dreams. I love you both with all of my heart.

CONTENTS

PART II: PHYSICAL BALANCE

PART III: INTELLECTUAL BALANCE

PART IV: EMOTIONAL BALANCE

FOREWORD

Joseph Murphy

In her marvelous guide to school leadership, Jan Irons Harris teaches us three valuable lessons. First, knowledge can be accumulated in an assortment of places, but wisdom can only be forged on the anvil of experience. Second, understanding, and especially understanding of one's self, is essential to effective leadership. And third, success as a person and as a school leader means maintaining balance in one's life. In her guide to balanced leadership, Dr. Harris speaks with wisdom and courage and an unfettered openness about lessons for us as school leaders. Her insights will touch your heart.

This is a wonderful book for many reasons. Most importantly, I think, because it provides a touchstone to navigate life as a school leader. As Dr. Harris reveals through her story, being a principal or assistant principal is a tough job. It is easy to lose one's way: to lose sight of the reason for taking on the work, to become dispirited and worn down, to become reactive, to assume the worst, and to lose joy. This is a book to help us stay grounded: to hold onto the good things, to travel the high road, and to do the right things. As such, it is a book full of wisdom.

At the same time, this is also a deeply warm book. Dr. Harris reminds us that school leadership is as much about the heart as it is the head. As such, the book goes a long way toward helping principals navigate the ethical and moral issues they confront. It does not offer a portfolio of answers so much as it helps us establish the principles we need to craft answers to the difficult problems and unclear opportunities that confront us. As such, it is a book of hope and possibilities.

Dr. Harris has also provided us with an amazingly accessible narrative. This is not a book of tables and figures. It is a volume of parables and stories—and deeply personal ones at that. For all the conversation about the importance of data-based *this* and evidence-based *that*, narrative remains central to the way we learn—and the narrative here is open, direct, personal, and deeply moving. As such, it is an amazing chronicle in which Dr. Harris touches each of us on a personal basis. There is more than a little stardust here.

Most books, even the best ones, are read and filed away. My hunch is that your relationship with this volume by Jan Irons Harris will be different. My guess is that you will revisit this guide to help influence the head and direct the heart throughout your journey in the principalship.

Joseph Murphy
Professor of Education and Associate Dean for Special Projects
Peabody College, Vanderbilt University

PREFACE

I am a teacher and I am proud to say so. For you see, the ability to teach is a gift from God, and I know that it is He who gave me this unique gift. Through the years, I have carefully used this precious gift in various capacities while serving as a secondary math teacher, high school assistant principal, middle school and high school principal, and, currently, as a superintendent in Cullman, Alabama. Prior to my appointment as superintendent, I served as a school administrator for more than sixteen years. During this time, I mentored teachers who aspired to become principals, and I also mentored new principals as they labored for success in their key leadership positions. I continue to do so at this time as well. As a result, I have presented, upon invitation, a number of training workshops for these leaders.

Serving as a principal is no easy task, as any past or present principal will tell you. It is often a thankless, exhausting job. When an acquaintance once asked me if I had a difficult job, I explained that my job could be described as "98 percent high-flying and 2 percent rock-bottom." This explanation captures my perception of life in the principal's office. The "rock-bottom" experiences have been few. Overall, the principalship has been rewarding for me, and I encourage its pursuit to leaders who long for the opportunity to make a difference in the lives of children. Serving as principal gives the educator the opportunity to lead efforts to create a vision, implement change, and, ultimately, positively improve the life of a child by creating learning environments that are inspiring and productive.

Dr. Earline Pinckley was my mentor. When I was a high school math teacher, Earline served as the assistant principal and voluntarily became my mentor without my knowledge. Upon realizing that I had a proclivity for school administration, she encouraged me to assume the journey to the principal's office. I did so, without hesitation, knowing it was the path I was destined to follow. As I approached the door to the principal's office, I struggled for a way to express my gratitude to Dr. Pinckley because I knew I could never repay her for her personal investment in my career. She told me she wanted no appreciation, only a promise that I, in turn, would help another educator find the road to the principal's office. I promised I would do so. The purpose of this simple book is to fulfill that promise.

This primer is a practical book. I am not an expert on any topic within it; I am a practitioner, not a scholar. This primer is designed to give the current or future principal simple words of wisdom from a person who knows what it is like to serve in the principal's office; I know the joys and sorrows, the successes and challenges of the principalship. This is a book that is filled with advice that I learned through the years by making mistakes, achieving success, and learning from others. I humbly offer this advice to you as I would offer it to a friend or colleague. I do not have all the answers; I am simply one who is willing to share lessons learned with others. Extract recommendations that speak to you as you create your unique leadership style. It is my genuine hope that this primer will serve as a helpful guide for leaders who long to experience a "high-flying" journey while in the principal's office.

ACKNOWLEDGMENTS

Heartfelt thanks to . . .

Dr. Tom Koerner and Paul Cacciato at Rowman & Littlefield for giving me the opportunity to publish my book. It has been a pleasure for me to work with these gentlemen, as well as Lynda Phung, my production editor.

Dr. Earline Pinckley for encouraging me to become a principal and mentoring me. She and Louise Amos taught me the ropes and then left Grissom High School to become successful middle school principals. Thank you, Louise and Earline.

The late Sid Ingram. I am indebted to Mr. Ingram; he hired me as a math teacher and then, later, as an assistant principal. I learned practical, powerful lessons from him. I am grateful that Mr. Ingram told Assistant Principal Doug Styles to train me when I became an assistant principal. Doug helped me to form my leadership style in the early years by teaching me and leading me. Thank you, Doug.

My former superintendents, Dr. Ron Saunders and Dr. Eugene Thompson, who selected me (after I was recommended by committee) to become a middle school and high school principal, respectively. It was an honor to serve as principal and work for them.

My professor, Dr. Joseph Murphy, for teaching and guiding me. Dr. Murphy is an inspiration to me. He is a brilliant man who radiates excellence and balance in his daily walk.

The Cullman City Board of Education for their support of my book-writing venture during my free time. I am truly blessed to work for President Suzanne Harbin, Vice-President Mark Bussman, Brenda Howell, Kaye Donnelly, and Dr. Jim Hoover. I am thankful that they gave me the opportunity to live my dream life in Cullman, Alabama.

Executive secretary Jackie Joiner. I am fortunate to work with her by my side each day; I could not survive without my sweet, intelligent Jackie. I love you like a sister.

My personal assistant, Amanda von Herrmann, who is an excellent editor and adviser. Amanda, I know that the "home office" put us together so that we could complete this work. Thank you for your dedication to detail. You are an amazing young woman.

My friends and family—especially my sister Rhonda Anderton—who encouraged me throughout the process as I worked to complete this book.

My parents, Bobby and Sara Irons, for their support and encouragement. I am thankful that God gave me these wonderful parents to provide a loving foundation for me and to help me to achieve my dreams.

My husband, Wholey. I especially thank you. During our marriage of twenty-five years, you have always encouraged me to pursue my dreams. You made a number of sacrifices so that I could write this book. Thank you, Wholey, for proofing my manuscript multiple times. Thank you for your prayers of blessing and also for your encouragement and strength. I love you. You are not only my husband—you are my best friend.

Finally, and most importantly, I thank God for the many blessings He gives me each day. I give the credit for any good that comes from this work to God Almighty for it is He that inspired me to write this book and gave me the strength and ability to create it.

INTRODUCTION

In order to be a successful principal, it is essential to look inward and obtain an understanding of self before attempting to lead others.

—Jan Irons Harris

Throughout my administrative career, I have mentored aspiring school administrators. Opportunities for me to share my knowledge with these future leaders came unsolicited. During these shared mentoring moments, I experienced an epiphany. I realized that these opportunities were perfectly in concert with my mission in life. I enjoyed sharing the techniques that I have found to work best in the principal's office because I knew I was passing on some of the most valuable lessons that we learn in life—the practical ones.

As I prepared for these teaching opportunities, I searched for a simple way to share the knowledge I had gained and a common theme emerged: *In order to be a successful principal, it is essential to look inward and obtain an understanding of self before attempting to lead others.*

PIES—THE FOUR AREAS OF OUR BEING

An understanding of one's self begins with an examination of the four areas of our being. These areas are the physical, intellectual, emotional, and spiritual parts of our existence. Some people refer to these areas by the acronym PIES. I find I can categorize each action in my life into one of these four domains. In fact, we can classify some actions in our lives into more than one domain. A good example of this is stress. It can affect one's physical as well as emotional well-being. Stress can also affect job performance or intellectual balance.

A few examples of activities that are classified in each area follow:

Physical: diet, exercise, sleep, grooming, posture, manners, communication
Intellectual: education, work, study, knowledge, organizing, analyzing, writing
Emotional: relationships, social events, self-esteem, stress, creativity, worry, forgiveness
Spiritual: mission, beliefs, values, worship, prayer, service, study

Once we understand and recognize these areas in our lives, we are then able to master strengths in each area, thereby creating a physically, intellectually, emotionally, and spiritually stronger being. In striving to achieve PIES balance, we are better equipped for success in the principal's office. For years, I have been telling others about the importance of maintaining PIES balance in order to obtain optimal success.

A Bicycle

Allow me to use a bicycle to assist me in my explanation. The bicycle must have two balanced wheels in order to work properly. Within the circumference of each wheel are spokes of equal length. The spokes divide the wheel into equal parts and this strengthens the wheel so that it does not collapse when the bike is in use. These equal parts could be viewed as the four parts of our being. This bicycle illustrates the importance of maintaining equal emphasis in each of the PIES areas in our lives. With an equally strong focus in each of these PIES areas, we can operate at our full potential and thus work efficiently like a properly balanced wheel that supports a bicycle.

In order to lead a balanced life, we must strengthen ourselves in each area and not lead a skewed life, for example, a life where work (Intellectual area) is the only thing of importance. Theoretically, each of the four areas should be given equal emphasis. From my personal experience and my observations, this seems to be a struggle for most people.

An Examination of Time Usage

A continual examination of the time I spend in each of the four PIES areas guides me in my selection of activities during free time. For example, if I have been working too many hours, I will often realize that it is time for play and initiate a game of tennis. I may realize that I have not spent enough time taking care of myself and dedicate an hour for a bubble bath and a manicure and pedicure, or I may dedicate a portion of my evening for a long walk while listening to my favorite music stored in my MP3 player. The bottom line is this—before I accept in-

Figure I.I.   Child's Art "Bicycle" by Beth Morris

vitations, watch television, or browse the Internet, I ask myself, "How do I want to spend my precious free time?" Posing this reflective question promotes more self-discipline and, in turn, a more balanced life.

It is helpful for me to reflect upon the state of my total condition by examining the percentage of time I spend in each or the four PIES areas. To demonstrate my thought process, let's look at the time we have in one week in table 1.1.

Table I.I.   Calculation for Free Time during One Week

Total time	24 hours in a day × 7 days a week	168 hours in a week
Sleep	8 hours a night × 7 nights	−56 hours
Work	40 hours per week	−40 hours
Commuting	4 hours per week*	−4 hours to and from work
Food preparation and eating	3 hours a day × 7 days	−21 hours
Grooming	I hour each day for × 7 days	−7 hours
Chores	estimate 6 hours a week	−6 hours
		=34 hours for free time

*On average, Americans spend 24 minutes commuting to work each day (according to the U.S. Census Bureau's press release "Americans Spend More Than 100 Hours Commuting to Work Each Year, Census Bureau Reports," dated March 30, 2005).
24 minutes to and from work, times five days a week = 240 minutes, or 4 hours.

Free Time

This liberal calculation allows time for sleep, work, food, grooming, and even chores—all of which are necessities for life. While your normal week may differ slightly from the allocations in my calculation, the point is that we all have approximately 34 hours of free time during each week or 4 hours and 51 minutes per day. Now, what do I do with the 34 hours of free time I have each week when I am not sleeping, working, preparing or eating food, grooming, doing chores, or taking care of family obligations such as children and/or aging parents? Do I work more than 40 hours a week? If so, I am reducing time that could be spent in the other three PIES areas. I am expending time and energy to work excessively when I need to use this valuable time for family, exercise, play, or spiritual growth. Another example might be spending extra time socializing or attending parties while neglecting the physical or spiritual parts of your being.

How much time do you spend in each of these four important areas? Do you spend time taking care of your emotional needs? Do you spend time nurturing your spiritual growth? Do you spend time developing a physically strong body? Likewise, do you intentionally allocate time to develop the intellectual part of your being?

THIS PRIMER

This primer is divided into four parts. It will begin with an examination of spiritual balance in the first part because spirituality provides our robust foundation. In part II, we will look at the importance of physical balance while recognizing the obvious fact that it is essential for us to take care of our basic physical needs and, for longevity, to exercise and eat well. The third section will analyze the importance of intellectual balance; it is imperative that we seek continual intellectual growth in order to be effective in the principal's office. And, finally, part IV will explore the need for emotional balance. As principal, you must be emotionally strong. It is a tough world and the weak will not survive.

This primer contains words of advice based on lessons that I have learned through my years of service. These recommendations are organized through each of the four areas in order to promote a realization of the need for balance in the physical, intellectual, emotional, and spiritual domains while serving in the principal's office. The four parts of our being are connected; they fit together like a puzzle. When all of these areas of our being are balanced and strong, we can more easily attain success in the principal's office.

I

SPIRITUAL BALANCE

The spiritual domain provides a foundation for all we say and do. It is comprised of our values, beliefs, worship, prayer, service, and study. It provides a basis from which we determine our mission and goals in life. It sustains us. It guides us. It comforts us when we fall. Regardless of your religious beliefs, it is fundamentally essential to maintain a proper focus in this area.

He that loseth wealth loseth much; he that loseth friends, loseth more; but he that loseth his spirit loseth all.

—Spanish Maxim in *Dictionary of Thoughts* (1877)

YOUR INTERNAL GLUE

Mission, Foundation, Values, Goals, and Beliefs

The nearest way to glory is to strive to be what you wish to be thought to be.

—Socrates

Each time I fly on a plane, I hear the flight attendant, while reviewing safety precautions, instruct parents to place oxygen masks on themselves prior to placing them on children in the event of an emergency. In other words, the flight attendant is advising the parents to help themselves before trying to help their children. If they do not follow this directive, their children could suffer as a result. As you begin or continue your journey as principal, help yourself before trying to help others by determining your personal mission or purpose in life. Additionally, seek to understand and define your foundation, values and beliefs. These important parts unite to form your internal glue in the spiritual domain. Together, they make you the unique person you are.

DETERMINE YOUR MISSION

Years ago, I found clarity in my professional and personal life by defining my "calling" or mission in life. My mission serves as a road map for my life. Determine your personal mission to help guide you through your life journey. Reflecting on questions may help you when you create your mission or calling. Some questions you may want to consider are:

- Where am I in my life journey?
- What do I want to accomplish with my life?
- What will be my legacy?

Answering these questions can be as difficult as pinning Jell-o to the wall, as the metaphor goes. In my quest to provide answers to these nagging questions, I find I am able to grasp this elusive concept best when I force myself to capture my thoughts and articulate them through a concise mantra known as a mission statement. Creating a mission statement is an arduous task, to say the least. It has taken me years to refine my mission statement; I have spent hours repeating the words within it until I was convinced that these words defined me as the person I am and the person I want to be. After reading the idea that Jesus had a mission in the book *Jesus, CEO*, by Laurie Beth Jones, and that it was to teach others a better way of life, I embraced this concept and adapted it as a starting point for my personal mission statement.

My mission is *to teach people a better way of life through love, education, and by example, utilizing my gifts of teaching and leading.*

Creating my mission statement forced me to define what is important in my life while recognizing the gifts I have been given to assist me in my journey. My mission statement is personal; it is my calling and it serves as a constant reminder of the person I want to be today and tomorrow. As a suggested resource for you, I found Stephen Covey's book, *The Seven Habits of Highly Effective People*, to be a helpful guide when writing my mission statement. Your mission statement will be an intimate part of your being once you define it and adopt it for your personal use.

Where there is no vision, the people perish.

—King Solomon, Proverbs 29:18 (KJV)

IDENTIFY THE COMPONENTS OF YOUR UNIQUE FOUNDATION

You may not realize it but, based on your background and experiences with others through your years of existence, your life is firmly based upon a foundation on which you perform your daily life tasks. This invisible foundation provides a basis for decision-making on every level.

As a newlywed, I took great pride in cooking for my husband, Wholey. A Southern girl, I certainly knew how to prepare delicacies such as cornbread and banana pudding. While preparing supper one night as I mixed the cornbread batter, I began to wonder why, after mixing all of the ingredients, I added a little water into the batter before pouring it into the iron skillet to bake. I called my mother to inquire why the recipe called for water. Her only explanation was that this is the way we do it. Alas, I later learned from my grandmother that she added a little water to the batter in an effort to stretch staples while feeding five hungry children during the Depression. For years, my mother, my sister and I had continued to follow the recipe without fully understanding it. We simply did what had been done previously and were pleased with the results.

The point of my story is to emphasize that we all have an operational foundation that is built with one brick at a time—through background and personal

---

Recipe: Virgie Irons's Cornbread

Put a small amount of butter or oil into an iron skillet. Place iron skillet in oven and pre-heat oven to 400°. In a large bowl, mix one egg with one cup of buttermilk with a whisk. Add one cup of self-rising cornmeal and 3/4 cup self-rising flour. Mix well. Add a little water while mixing. Carefully pour batter into hot skillet (do not spatter the hot oil on you) and bake 25 minutes or so. Brown the cornbread by broiling it in the oven for a few minutes, if necessary. When done, turn cornbread onto a plate and slice into pie pieces for supper. Yields one pan of cornbread (about eight slices).

---

experiences. This foundation is just as unique as your fingerprint. It includes your family and your education, your friends and personal experiences. In short, it represents who you are and where you have been.

Before you begin your journey as principal, determine the unique ingredients that make up your foundation, because you will be tested like never before in this new leadership capacity. Remove or renovate any part of your foundation that does not accurately reflect the person you want to be. You are not your grandmother. You are a unique individual. If you have not already done so, it is time to define your personal values and beliefs that make the unique foundation on which you have built your life.

WHAT VALUES ARE PACKED IN YOUR LITTLE SUITCASE?

When I was a little girl, I had a petite, red suitcase that I carried with me when I visited my grandparents and went on family trips; I still have this treasured artifact. My little suitcase is approximately 12 inches long, 12 inches wide, and 8 inches deep. It displays an appliqué of a hip teenager on the top beneath the handle. Upon opening the suitcase, a mounted mirror is revealed in its interior. When I was young, I enjoyed carefully packing special toys and other items in this adorable suitcase.

I use this little red suitcase as a visual aid when I speak to students as they are about to transition from elementary school to middle school or from middle school to high school. I place certain items in my little suitcase and talk to my students

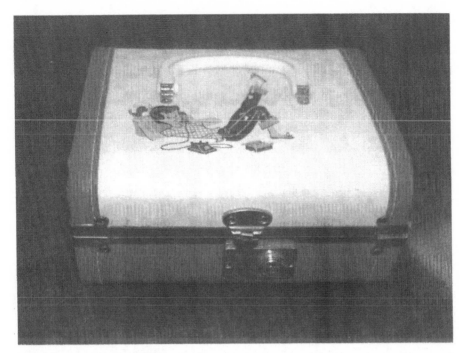

Figure 1.1. Little Red Suitcase

about each item. Some of the items I include, for example, are my baby shoes (remember where you have been), a photo of my parents (take your parents with you—talk to them—they love you more than anyone else), and a road map (have a plan—know where you are going).

We all have an imaginary suitcase that we carry from birth with us everywhere we go. Others place items in our little suitcase through the years. These items include values or ideals that our loved ones want us to embrace as our own as we mature. At some point during adolescence or early adulthood, we examine the values in our little suitcase and start the cleaning out process. We decide for ourselves if we want to continue to hold certain values in our suitcase. As we examine each value, we either return the value back to the suitcase or discard it. Often, we carry extra weight in our suitcase simply because we do not wish to examine a particular value. In order to define our personal values, we must examine the contents of our suitcase and determine which values will remain and which values are discarded.

What values are packed in your little suitcase? A few of the values I have in my little suitcase include honesty, compassion, love, and submission to authority. For example, I strongly believe in submitting to authority. It is a biblical concept and it parallels my view of essential values needed in order to live in a civilized society. If you don't think authority, rules, and order are important, you might want to read *Lord of the Flies* by William Golding to see what can happen when order dissipates in a crisis situation. Because of this value, I subject myself to authority by obeying our laws, just as I expect students to obey the school rules and their teachers. Because I view schools as miniature worlds for children where we are preparing them to be productive citizens one day, it is important to me to teach students this value by establishing and supporting both rules and the authority of teachers.

I encourage you to determine now what's packed in your little suitcase. These values will be part of your foundation as you serve as the instructional, moral leader of your school. Thinking about it now will help to prepare you as you begin your service as the "judge" in important matters at your school.

It's not hard to make decisions when you know what your values are.

—Roy Disney

CREATE GOALS

There are those that look at things the way they are, and ask "why?" I dream of things that never were, and ask "why not?"

—Robert F. Kennedy

By having a spiritual foundation in place, we are then able to move toward the realization of our potential. The best way to seek optimal realization of capabilities is through the use of goals. Henry David Thoreau said, "Go confidently in the direction of your dreams. Live the life you imagined." To go confidently in the direction of your dreams, you must first define the dreams or goals you desire. Then, move toward these goals.

When I was a teenager, on one New Year's Eve, my youth minister gave my friends and me an assignment. We were told to write our short-term and long-term goals on a piece of paper. We were encouraged to define our goals for the upcoming new year, goals for five years, and, finally, long-term goals for ten years. I enjoyed the exercise because it forced me to think about what I wanted to do with my life. During that same time period, my middle school English teacher required us to keep a journal. It was at this time that I began keeping a personal journal. I continue to maintain a journal to record my goals and thoughts. More than twenty-five years ago, I wrote in my journal:

GOALS

Get married
Get master's degree
Get doctorate
Buy a house

—Jan Irons Harris, January 27, 1982

When I completed my doctorate, I received congratulations from my professor, Dr. Joseph Murphy, who asked me what I was thinking about at that moment. I told him I had written in my journal many years before that I wanted to obtain my doctorate one day. I told him it felt great to complete my degree and accomplish this important goal today.

Declaring and reviewing goals helps you to make these goals become a reality. Having a goal is like having and following a road map; it helps you to stay on track and reach your final destination. It is not enough to simply state goals. We must review them periodically and bring them to life through our conversations with others. In the absence of goals, time can slip by and leave us wondering where the years went and why we did not accomplish anything of significance. It is so easy to stay in the same daily routine and not push ourselves to improve each day.

How Do You Eat an Elephant?

As I consider goal-setting, I am reminded of the question, "How do you eat an elephant?" Answer: "One bite at a time." I claim this mantra when working on various projects at home or at work. I can accomplish much if I break the big project into "bite-sized" pieces that are not overwhelming for me to tackle. Feeling a sense of accomplishment after I finish a bite-sized piece also encourages me to keep going. I often remembered this philosophy when I was in graduate school while working full-time. It was a challenging time for me because of the time constraints—but I knew that if I could keep "eating one bite at a time" that I would achieve my goal to complete my doctorate. And this is what I did. This is also how I wrote this book, one page at a time.

It is imperative that as the school leader, you identify your personal goals and then identify your school goals. Once defined, communicate these goals and make them a reality for your school even if it means separating them into smaller, quicker-to-attain goals that will keep you on track. Goals are part of the strategic planning process. They guide the principal when making future decisions about facilities and curriculum.

If you want to live a happy life, tie it to a goal and not to people or things.

—Albert Einstein

BELIEFS

When I completed my doctorate at Vanderbilt University, one of my colleagues, Deborah McLachlin, gave me a beautiful, wooden kaleidoscope to commemorate this significant milestone in my life. While I viewed the light through the lens of this thoughtful gift, Deborah explained that, like a kaleidoscope, education changes the lens through which we view the world. My friend wanted me to have this unique gift as a reminder that we would now see the world in a different light after our shared educational experience.

Through Which Lens Do You View the World?

Each person views the world through a unique lens just as an individual who wears eyeglasses has a perfect, customized prescription that enables the person to see properly. And so it is with beliefs. Each person views the world through a unique lens based on their background, experiences, and values. Through this view, each person's beliefs are determined.

For example, one of my former students, Amanda, was uncomfortable with her teacher because the teacher had a loud voice. She viewed this teacher's loud voice as a source of intimidation because she came from an abusive home. Because this student was intimidated by this teacher, she believed the teacher did not like her. I received no other complaints about this teacher which led me to believe this complaint was the anomaly. This experience reminds us that each of us has a unique view of the world: One student might not be offended by a loud voice, whereas another student might be frightened because of his or her past experience.

Prejudices also alter a person's view of the world and thereby will affect his or her beliefs. Stereotypes based on prejudices can only damage relationships in a school. We must seek to avoid prejudices and stereotypes at all costs. Stereotypes are not truth, just as appearances are not truth. For example, one of my favorite students was most intimidating in his physical appearance. He was a tall, muscular, young man who wore baggy pants and gang paraphernalia. I can understand why any person who did not know him would be afraid to approach him. Truthfully, he had his share of disciplinary infractions, but he consistently presented himself as controlled and mannerly to me. I knew his family and was not afraid of this student. I saw this young man at the shopping mall one night while I was with a friend. The young man came over and spoke to me and was pleasant and kind. My friend was frightened by his appearance.

On the other hand, I can also recall a small, young woman who was a student at the high school when I served as principal. This female looked like the model student. However, she was one of the meanest students with whom I ever worked. She engaged in a fight at school one day and our school resource officer had to handcuff her in order to remove her from the school because she was totally out of control. Even though this small girl could not possibly weigh 100 pounds, she was not to be trusted. Appearances are deceiving.

Through which lens do you view the world? Do you view the world with a positive, optimistic attitude? Do you believe the glass is half full or half empty? Do you strive to believe the best about people instead of the worst? Do you give people the benefit of the doubt? The lens through which I choose to view the world is an optimistic one. I choose to believe the best about people at all times until they give me a reason not to believe them. I hope that others will, in turn, give me the benefit of the doubt, too.

YOUR INTERNAL GLUE

Your internal glue is comprised of your mission, foundation, values, goals, and be-liefs. Together, these components sustain and guide you. These elements keep you "together"—just like glue. Your mission is your purpose in life; it guides you and helps you to make personal decisions. Your foundation is determined by your background and experiences. It helps to establish your beliefs and values. After recognizing these important components in your foundation, you are able to insti-tute goals and make plans for your future. Be able to express your customized de-scription of these elements so that they describe you perfectly.

(2)

RENEW AND REFINE

Strengthen Your Internal Glue

The unexamined life is not worth living.

—Socrates

Renewal and refinement go hand in hand in your quest to continually improve. Each day, you must find time to renew your spirit. Each day, you must examine your life and look for ways to hone your actions so that you continually improve. Be faithful to this practice of renewal and refinement and you will enhance your effectiveness as principal.

RENEW

It is necessary to seek continual renewal in order to maintain health, happiness, and sanity while in the principal's office. Each person has his or her unique way of recharging the internal batteries, and it is imperative that you find a personalized way to do so. In our daily lives, we expend energy from our spiritual reservoir as we help others. We replenish this spiritual energy through daily renewal. If you do not welcome this practice, your energy reservoir will soon be depleted and you may experience stress, illness, or exhaustion. Some simple things that I try to do to renew myself daily include reading some of my favorite Bible verses in the morning at home before I get my day started; sitting at rest at my desk for a few quiet moments during the day to reflect on what I have ahead of me; or just getting up from my desk and taking a short walk to collect my thoughts.

I learned firsthand what could happen when we do not make time for renewal. When I was a high school principal, I recall a stressful time I experienced during the building of a new high school on the campus that housed the old school. Due to a number of circumstances beyond my control, I was loaded with responsibility and stress. As a result, I began to have difficulty swallowing. I went to see my doctor who told me that I was fine and that this symptom was a manifestation of stress. Her simple advice was for me to slow down and "just breathe."

It was at this time that I realized the importance of daily renewal. I was so busy at school that I ignored the ritual of daily renewal. During stressful times, the need for renewal is paramount. Do not neglect renewal activities during these times. Today, I recognize the tightness in my throat as a physical sign that I need to slow down and "just breathe." Do not wait until you have a physical sign of stress. Proactively seek daily renewal in order to manage the stressful job in the principal's office.

First Steps

How do you renew your spirit? The first step for daily renewal is a realization that time is essential for this daily ritual. You must dedicate a few minutes each day for renewal. Remember that even just fifteen minutes a day for renewal is better than zero minutes a day for renewal. Stop racing long enough so that you can take a few minutes for rejuvenation. Let's be candid: Most of us are pounded with stimuli from the time our feet touch the floor in the morning until we drop exhausted into the bed at night. When we have fifteen minutes of free time, usually the television or music is blaring, someone is talking to us, or we are running to the computer to check our email. If you want to renew your spirit, you must create specific time to do so.

Take a few minutes to embrace silence and just "be." Do not automatically turn on the radio or music in the car. Perhaps this is a good time for silent reflection as you travel from one location to another—whether in the morning, during the day, or at night. When you awaken, do not automatically turn on the television or race to check your email. Instead, welcome silence and enjoy nature's sounds. I thoroughly enjoy listening to the birds sing in the early morning hours; I take the time to watch them feed in our garden, where we provide food for them throughout the year. In fact, we added a storm door in our family room so that we could watch our little friends come and go.

My Favorite Things

On November 1, 1996, while embracing silence, I began to think about my favorite things in life. I decided to make a list of my favorite things and record them for posterity in my journal. This personal list was entitled "My Favorite Things."

Just tonight I was thinking about the sweetest gifts of life that I enjoy. First, I enjoy excellent health and a fine husband, family, and friends. I am blessed to be able to walk and run and participate in athletic endeavors. Each new day that I awake in our home in Huntsville, I appreciate the mountains which surround our lovely home. Today the leaves are in their splendor—all colors are apparent as they prepare for their descent to the earth. The sky is so beautiful with cotton-puff clouds scattered about. Each sunset is a thankful gift. I love awakening my senses and enjoying the awareness of being truly alive. I like the "smells" of campfires, cookouts, flowers, and grass. I love to feel the breeze upon my face and hear the wind chimes on my front porch gently make their melodious song. I love anticipating a great, long-awaited meal. I enjoy a good night's sleep and love awakening in a cool, sun-filled bedroom with birds singing outside my windowpane. I love sleeping while the rain softly falls upon the roof and trees. I love my kitty cat and the calmness she gives me as I hold her in my lap and stroke her while she purrs. I love to recognize and appreciate differences among all people. It makes me all the more thankful for who I am and where I am in my journey through life. I see more each day that life and death are separated by a narrow margin. When I am with my husband, I love to see and feel his strength. He is my protector, my strength, and my friend. I love life and enjoy these things I've listed. God gives many gifts to us daily. I will never take any for granted.

What are your favorite things? What makes you feel peaceful and happy? Define your favorite things in life and record them in your journal. After you list your favorite things, make time to enjoy them in order to renew your spirit by scheduling them in your calendar in the same way that you would schedule a dental appointment. Make time to fire up the grill if you enjoy a meal outdoors. If you enjoy picnics, schedule a time for a family picnic. If you enjoy listening to wind chimes, then purchase wind chimes, hang them, and be still and silent long enough to enjoy their song.

FIND THE TIME AND PLACE TO THINK, PRAY, AND STUDY

I enjoy rising before the sun comes up. When I was in my twenties, I remember staying up until 11:00 p.m. or so each night. I also remember how difficult it was to get up in the morning! I was always tired and rushed to get dressed and out the door. Because I now realize the benefit of an "early to bed and early to rise" lifestyle, I find the morning to be the most glorious part of my day! During this time, I like to think, pray, study, and write. I enjoy reading a chapter of the book of Proverbs each day especially because there are thirty-one chapters in the book. I read the chapter of Proverbs that corresponds to the day of the month. The book of Proverbs is filled with wisdom from King Solomon, the richest and wisest man who ever lived. One of my favorite verses in Proverbs comes from chapter 3, verses 5 and 6: *Trust in the Lord with all your heart and lean not on your own understanding; in all your ways acknowledge him, and he will make your paths straight* (NIV).

Other Times for Quiet Reflection

An "early to bed and early to rise" approach is certainly one way to allow time in the mornings for renewal and refinement. However, if you do not take advantage of the early hours, and many of us cannot due to responsibilities with children and other family members, then find another time for quiet reflection. Perhaps this time is in the afternoon. A teacher and friend with whom I worked at Whitesburg Middle School embraced this same ritual when she arrived home in the afternoon. Bonnie Hamner and her late husband enjoyed a pot of coffee when she entered the sanctuary of her home at the end of each day. This enabled her to slow down and enjoy this treat before beginning to cook supper or complete any other task she had yet to accomplish. Bonnie also enlisted the use of her fine china to help make this practice even more extraordinary.

How do you find time to relax and renew? It makes no difference if your time for reflection is during the morning, afternoon, or night. It is only important that you create time for this valuable practice in your daily schedule. Commit to make a plan so that you can begin this practice today.

Dedicate a Special Place to Think, Pray, and Study

> . . . a prudent man gives thought to his steps.
>
> —King Solomon, Proverbs 14:15 (NIV)

After you find the time to think, pray, and study, you must find a special place that will enhance your practice. My friend Johanna Habisreitinger dedicates a special place in her home as her spiritual space. This special place is located in her bedroom where she has a comfortable chair with a table beside it. A pretty lamp sits on the table to aid her efforts to read and study. Religious artifacts lay on the table. Her Bible is located here along with an inspirational book, a small cross, and a candle. She has a lovely white tablecloth on the table. This is where she enjoys a few minutes of meditation, prayer, and study each morning. This is where she can think. This special place is like a baby blanket that encases her as she takes time to reflect.

Where do you go to think, pray, and study? I find having a dedicated space for this beneficial activity to be soothing and comforting. I have a special club chair in my great room that I enjoy using because of the comfort of the chair and the light that surrounds me in this location. At times, I will go to this chair in the early morning hours before the sun rises to reflect upon decisions I must make. I will often pray and study here, as well as write in my journal. I keep a chenille throw blanket over the ottoman to use in the chilly mornings.

At my previous house, I had a delightful swing on my back screened porch and a double rocker on my covered front porch. I enjoyed these locations morning, noon, and night. Fluffy, comfortable pillows were in both spots. Monstrous trees surrounded our house and provided a privacy screen—because of this, I was able to retreat to either of these locations in the early hours to read, reflect, and pray while still in my pajamas. In the fall and early spring chilly mornings, I loved to wrap up in my grandmother's quilt while sitting there and enjoying a cup of steaming hot coffee while renewing my spirit. I wrote about that special quilt on March 11, 1988:

My grandmother's quilt reminds me
of the love that we did share
Like her presence, it protects me
from the winter, cold night air
It's made with many fabrics
from clothes she made for my dolls and me
Like the many times we shared,
memories I vividly see
My grandmother's quilt
is worn and fragile because it's old
Like my grandmother's life,
what a story her days have told
The colors now are faded
from sunlight and from age
Like a book revealing secrets,
I am absorbing every page
My grandmother's quilt is an heirloom
I shall give to my child from me
I will tell of special memories,
what a treasure the quilt will always be
And though she is here no longer,
through her quilt, she still speaks to me
I will always remember my grandmother
and the love she gave to me

Use Special Items to Assist You in Your Quest for Renewal

Just as I use and enjoy my grandmother's quilt during my times of renewal, I encourage you to use the special items you have each day to renew your spirit; do not put all your special treasures away for safekeeping. Use the gifts that are given to you! Enjoy them as you enjoy life each day! For example, use your favorite coffee cup or fine china instead of the faded mug. Use your best tablecloth or heirloom quilt if it renews your spirit while using it. These items were intended for your pleasure, so enjoy them!

Other Places to Think, Pray, and Study

Of course, you are not limited to the confines of your house to find a dedicated space to think, pray, and study. Your dedicated space could be in the woods, along the river, or even on the golf course because each person has his or her own special interests. At one time, we had a tiny cabin on Smith Lake. One of my favorite activities was to get on my jet ski and ride to the middle of the lake while the sun was coming up. It was glorious! I remember singing "How Great Thou Art" loudly—right there in the middle of Smith Lake! (No one could hear me!) This is a joyous memory I will treasure forever. Having a dedicated place to renew your spirit—whether it is inside your house or on the lake or golf course—will help you with the heavy load you will carry at times, as principal.

My point is simple. Find a dedicated space to renew your spirit. Do you have a dedicated space for renewal? Do you allow time to renew your spirit? Having this time enables you to think about major decisions coming your way in the near future. Having this time enables you to relax and give your problems to God instead of carrying them all day long on your shoulders. Having this time enables you to find balance.

KEEP A JOURNAL

Purchase a journal to assist you in your time of thinking, prayer and study. Date your entries and record spontaneous thoughts and observations in your journal. You will reflect upon your journal entries from time to time and see the growth you have made through the years.

Figure 2.1. Child's Art "Read and Relax," by Cort Chandler

Make a Prayer of Thanksgiving or Petition

You might find it refreshing to also write a personal prayer in your journal. It could be a prayer of petition or thanksgiving. I found it helpful to create my personal prayer. One prayer I wrote on March 2, 2006, follows:

Father, be alive in me.
Wash my mistakes away with your blood;
through forgiveness, make me holy
Help me to live with a thankful, forgiving heart
Bless my family and me, O Lord, I pray
Protect us from evil

Father, be alive in me
Take my life and lead me
Help me pay attention and listen to you
Let me be your arms and legs
when delivering kindness and love unto others
Protect me from laziness and lack of self-discipline

Father, be alive in me
Walk with me everywhere I go;
never leave me
Let me always feel your presence
While I am alive on this earth,
grant me wisdom and knowledge like Solomon
Protect me as I travel through life unto death;
let me know you are with me

Father, be alive in me
Help me to be a good steward
of the gifts you give to me
Make me see with amazement
the beauty of your creation
Make me aware that we are only here a
short time in this temporary home
Protect the little children,
the weak and the strong from the evil one

Father, be alive in me
Give me faith like Job,
and courage like David
Give me the gift of leadership like Joshua,
and love like Mary
Help me to carry your illuminated message
of love and hope wherever I go
Protect me, Lord.

Figure 2.2.   Poem: "Father Be Alive in Me"

At times, I will simply read this prayer instead of creating a new prayer. A prayer can also be a single word such as "Thanks!" or "Help!," or it can be a long list of requests such as the one I shared. A down-to-earth prayer may be one such as, "Guide and protect me today." An uncomplicated prayer may be a verse from the Bible that gives you strength and encouragement. One of my favorite verses that I use as a simple prayer is located in Psalm 143:10: *Teach me to do your will, for you are my God; may your good Spirit lead me on level ground* (NIV). Prayer gives us strength and helps us by empowering us to do the job ahead of us. I could not have served as principal without the tool of prayer.

Jesus often withdrew to lonely places and prayed.

—Luke 5:16 (NIV)

REFINE

In order to strengthen your internal glue, it is critical to seek spiritual refinement along with renewal in order to perform at the highest level possible while in the principal's office. During these moments of renewal, examine your strengths and weaknesses. Determine the areas in which you need to improve. For example, you may reflect upon the way in which you handled a discipline case at your school and find ways to improve in the future. Each person is unique; each person has different weaknesses. If you are unsure of the areas in which you need to improve, you might digest the following questions to help you discover weaknesses:

- How have I encouraged others this week?
- Did I control my temper this week?
- Have I thought before I spoke this week?
- Did I make anyone feel better about himself or herself this week?
- Did I make a friend this week by truly listening and helping another person?
- Did I make an enemy this week? If yes, why? How could I have handled this situation better?

- What positive character traits can others see in me on a daily basis?
- What do I want people to remember about me after I leave this office?

Once you identify a spiritual area that needs refinement, you can begin working to improve in this area. For example, if you discover, upon reflection, that you were unkind to a student or employee because that person has treated you unfairly, perhaps you need to read and study (during your renewal time) about forgiveness. If you realize you have not encouraged others, perhaps you need to incorporate some simple ideas or habits into your daily routine to improve in this area. A couple of my favorite books include Joel Osteen's book, *Your Best Life Now*, and Richard Foster's books, *Celebration of Discipline* and *Prayer*.

RENEWAL AND REFINEMENT ARE MARRIED

Spiritual renewal and refinement are married; they go together. Seek continual renewal and improvement each day and you will witness accelerated spiritual growth that will further equip you for the important responsibilities you carry in the principal's office.

3

SEPARATE CHURCH AND STATE

Congress shall make no law respecting an establishment of religion, or prohibiting the free exercise thereof; or abridging the freedom of speech, or of the press; or the right of the people peaceably to assemble, and to petition the government for a redress of grievances.

—The First Amendment

The issue of "separation of church and state," derived from the first amendment, is a popular topic of conversation in today's world. For example, in the April 2, 2007 issue of *Time*, the cover reads "Why We Should Teach the Bible in Public School, But Very, Very Carefully." This issue highlights the fact that it is legal to teach the Bible as long as you do not proselytize. I used this issue of *Time* magazine for a Bible study class one Sunday. Because of the abundance of comments and questions generated by this interesting publication, the lesson was extended for two weeks instead of one.

A BASIC UNDERSTANDING OF THE BIBLE

This issue of *Time* explains that in order to be a well-rounded, educated individual, it is imperative to have a basic understanding of the Bible because of the many allusions to the Bible in literature. Additionally, daily conversations often reference characters and events that can be found in this bestselling book of all time. Further, the publication argues students can and should be taught about the Bible. It states that complications only arise when teachers drift from teaching the Bible to preaching beliefs.

The Golden Rule

In Alabama, the Bible provides the foundation for our character education program in that we are mandated, by state statute, to teach the Golden Rule. This universal rule, known as "the ethic of reciprocity" in different religions and cultures, is "to treat others the way you want to be treated." This golden rule comes from the Bible and can be found in Matthew 7:12, where it states: "So in everything, do to others what you would have them do to you, for this sums up the Law and the Prophets." Luke 6:31 states: "Do to others as you would have them do to you" (NIV). I will discuss the golden rule in more detail in Chapter 5.

Little Jezebel

Embedded within our daily conversations are various references to stories found in the Bible. For example, a colleague told me he was concerned about his son because he was dating a "little Jezebel." Because I was raised in a Christian family that attended a Bible-based church three times a week, I immediately understood his reference. However, others may not understand this reference without familiarity of the Bible. The story of Jezebel, who was married to King Ahab, can be found in the Old Testament of the Bible. One key verse from 1 Kings 21:25 follows: "There was never a man like Ahab, who sold himself to do evil in the eyes of the Lord, urged on by Jezebel his wife" (NIV).

I understood my colleague's message; he did not like the girl his son was dating since he called her by the name Jezebel. The name of Jezebel has a negative connotation because it implies that the woman is manipulative or sexually immoral. Jezebel initiated child sacrifices and sexual immorality as well as the worship of idols. If I had not possessed a basic understanding of the Bible, I would have been uneducated in this conversation and had no clue to the intent of my colleague's message.

Doubting Thomas

Another example of biblical references is when a person says, "He is a doubting Thomas." The phrase "Doubting Thomas" comes from the New Testament, where we learn that the apostle Thomas would not believe something unless he experienced the information firsthand. He was a "doubter." Thomas did not believe the other apostles when they told him they had seen the risen Lord.

The story of Thomas's "doubting" can be found in Luke 20:24–29:

Now Thomas (called Didymus), one of the Twelve, was not with the disciples when Jesus came. So the other disciples told him, "We have seen the Lord!" But he said to them, "Unless I see the nail marks in his hands and put my finger where the nails were, and put my hand into his side, I will not believe it." A week later his disciples were in the house again and Thomas was with them. Though the doors were locked, Jesus came and stood among them and said, "Peace be with you!" Then he said to

Thomas, "Put your finger here; see my hands. Reach out your hand and put it into my side. Stop doubting and believe." Thomas said to him, "My Lord and my God!" Then Jesus told him, "Because you have seen me, you have believed; blessed are those who have not seen and yet have believed." (NIV)

QUOTING THE BIBLE PUBLICLY

From time to time, I will use Bible verses in my speeches. When I spoke to sixth, seventh, and eighth graders about making good choices, I used Joshua, a leader in the Old Testament of the Bible, as an example of a man who made good choices. I quoted this verse from the Old Testament in Joshua 24:15: "And if it seems evil unto you to serve the LORD, choose you this day whom ye will serve; whether the gods which your fathers served that were on the other side of the flood, or the gods of the Amorites, in whose land ye dwell but as for me and my house, we will serve the LORD" (KJV).

In addition to quoting verses from the Bible that relate to my comments, I may also quote presidents and other great leaders. When preparing my remarks, if I think of a perfect reference, whether it is from the Bible or not, I do not hesitate to use it if it fits my message. I do not, however, use this opportunity to proselytize. Therein is the difference.

CHURCH ACTIVITIES AT SCHOOL

Most public schools do not teach the Bible. Legislators have had lengthy debates about whether or not they should allow Bible classes to be taught in secular schools. In our country, school activities have emerged such as the "Moment of Silent Reflection" at the start of the day or "Meet You at the Pole" where students peacefully assemble before school and pray around the flagpole. Additionally, Christian clubs such as the Fellowship of Christian Athletes can be found in most any school in America.

It is common for me to encounter members of the community during daily activities and find that religious conversations emerge from these individuals' comments and questions. Through the years, numerous individuals have given materials to me related to the issue of church and state. These citizens express concern over their perceived lack of religious freedom of students. It has been my experience to discover that many people are interested in this misunderstood topic.

SEPARATE CHURCH AND STATE?

How does the issue of separation of church and state relate to you while you are serving in the principal's office? It is imperative that you remember to "separate church and state." It is essential that you know what your beliefs are (church) and that you understand what actions are in accordance with the laws that exist in the United States of America (state). Let me explain with a true story.

When I served as a high school principal, a young woman came to see me to request permission to start a Wiccan club at our school. I listened intently as she communicated her desire to me. When she finished speaking, I asked her if her parents were aware of her proposal to start this club. She indicated that they were aware of her proposal and fully supported her efforts. I then asked her if she had a faculty sponsor for this proposed club. She stated that she did not. I told her the first step to forming a new club was obtaining a faculty sponsor. I told her to let me know when she found a teacher who would be willing to sponsor the club. My answer was not related to my spiritual beliefs; I provided a response based on the law. My religious beliefs had nothing to do with the legal answer I provided to this student.

Be spiritually strong. Define your beliefs, but know the difference between what you personally believe and what the Supreme Court rules. Separate church and state. Do not confuse what you believe and what you know is law. Beware— this can easily happen without you meaning to do it if you have a strong belief system. Do not discriminate against a person because he/she holds a different view than you do. Do not force your views upon those whom you supervise. I make it a practice to avoid conversations about politics and religion at work.

> *Believing that religion is a matter which lies solely between man and his God, that he owes account to none other for his faith or his worship, that the legislative powers of government reach actions only, and not opinions, I contemplate with sovereign reverence that act of the whole American people which declared that their Legislature should "make no law respecting an establishment of religion, or prohibiting the free exercise thereof," thus building a wall of separation between Church and State.*

> —Thomas Jefferson, Letter to the Danbury Baptists, 1802

4

PROACTIVITY

Avoid Potholes with Accountability and Guidance from a Mentor

Know when to ask for advice and when to take it.

—Dr. Ron Saunders, Superintendent

When I am driving down the road and I see a pothole, I do my best to safely avoid it. I know by going through the pothole I may damage my car or jeopardize my wheel alignment. City road crews do their best to keep potholes repaired for maximum safety, but because it is a continual process for road crews, they are not able to keep all the potholes filled all the time. Potholes are a reality of life. My niece, Shelly Cain, says repeatedly "Pay attention." We need to pay attention when driving so we can avoid accidents and potholes and be aware when emergency vehicles are approaching. Avoiding the pothole may take only a second, but not paying attention may mean spending a lot of my time and money having my car repaired.

POTHOLES IN THE PRINCIPAL'S OFFICE

In the principal's office, there are also potholes. We read about these potholes in the daily newspaper and on the Internet, and hear about them on the television's nightly news. Some of the potholes I have seen principals go through in my career include:

- Mismanagement of money
- Inappropriate relationships with students
- Inappropriate relationships with employees

- Misuse of public property
- Illegal substance use on school property
- Misuse of vacation, personal, and sick leave
- Submission of dishonest expense reimbursement forms

These potholes can quickly ruin one's career, as well as his or her personal life. Avoid these and other potholes at all costs, especially by adopting a proactive attitude. The first proactive step to take is to acknowledge that these potholes exist. Acknowledge that you are a human being with weaknesses and vulnerabilities. Then, seek accountability in all your actions. Being proactive and accountable are ways to avoid spending all of your time dealing with the aftermath of a pothole. Finally, enlist the guidance of a trusted mentor whom you can call on when you need to discuss an issue before acting on it.

ACCOUNTABILITY

Be accountable at all times. Let me repeat this again. Be accountable at all times. Be transparent in all your actions. A few examples of transparency and accountability follow.

Put a glass window pane in your office door so that your assistant can see if you are in your office and if you are with someone. You are at risk in your office when you close the door and you are alone with a student, parent, or employee. For example, a male colleague told me about a female being in his office and leaning over his desk in a revealing manner. It terrified him that she could leave his office and say basically anything she wanted about what happened behind the closed door. It would be her word against his word. Just this week, I heard on the news that a high school assistant principal was arrested due to alleged sexual misconduct with a teenaged student in his office. At Grissom High School, where I served as an assistant principal, this would be impossible because of the accountability we had in place with the windows in the office doors.

Avoid situations with an adult or student that could put you in an awkward or tempting position. Once, I was scheduled to carpool to a meeting out of town with three other principals. As it turned out, some of the principals had conflicts and were unable to go on the trip. As a result, it was going to be just one male principal and me going to the meeting. I declined going as well simply because it made me uncomfortable to ride for several hours in the car with just the two of us. Also, I did not want to check into the hotel with just the two of us. I do not put myself in a situation that makes me uncomfortable. You may disagree with my decision in this instance, but I prefer to avoid potential problem situations rather than deal with them afterward.

Tell your assistant your schedule at all times. It is courteous to communicate your whereabouts during the day to your assistant. I use Microsoft Outlook to keep my schedule and share it with my assistant. I also like to simultaneously keep a paper calendar. In addition to these two time management tools, I also tell my assistant where I am going and when I plan to return as I leave my office. Think about the response you are forcing your assistant to give to those who come to see you when you are out of the office. Which sounds professional and appropriate?

- I'm sorry, but Dr. Harris is not in. I will be happy to give her a message whenever she returns, if you like.
- I'm sorry, but Dr. Harris is not in. She is conducting a teacher evaluation this morning and is in the classroom. She should return around 11:00 a.m. I will be happy to give her a message when she returns, if you would like.

Complete leave forms promptly and accurately, and submit them to your assistant to process.   By doing so, your assistant sees firsthand that you are honest. If you are taking planned leave, make sure you turn in a leave form to your assistant prior to taking the leave. If it is unplanned leave, fill out a leave form the first day you return to the office. I have heard office staff members bitterly complain that the principal does not have to take vacation or sick leave. When you are out of the office, fill out the proper form and give it to your assistant so that he or she will see it. Be transparent so that those with whom you work will respect the fact that you are honest and accountable.

Complete expense forms honestly and accurately.   I will never forget being at a state meeting when the leader distributed expense forms for mileage reimbursement. Before the meeting began, I had seen a group of individuals get out of the car together and so I knew that they had carpooled to this meeting. Even so, each one of them completed a form, submitted it for mileage reimbursement and then joked about it afterward. This was alarming to me because I hold the view that if you cannot be trusted in small matters, you cannot be trusted in big matters. Taking the $40 mileage reimbursement was wrong and I lost respect for these individuals as a result of it. Remember that your character is displayed in small matters just as much as in big matters.

Never use school assets for personal reasons.   For example, if you have materials leftover after a building project, do not take these materials home. If you need staples or paper at home, do not take supplies from the office to your home for personal use. Keep school assets at school.

Be vigilant when handling school money.   Always have two people present when counting money. Deposit cash at the bank daily. Supervise those individuals charged with the responsibility for handling money watchfully.

Have a good attitude when someone asks you a question.   Do not be defensive and take the position that you are the principal and therefore answer to no one. We all are accountable. Make all decisions as if you had to explain your actions before the board of education or as if a story was to be printed on the front page of your local newspaper.

SEEK GUIDANCE FROM A MENTOR WHEN NEEDED

Plans fail for lack of counsel, but with many advisers they succeed.

—King Solomon, Proverbs 15:22 (NIV)

If you do not have a mentor in your field, actively seek a mentor today. Look for a wise, successful administrator who you respect and trust. Ask this person if he/she would be willing to mentor you. This person will be honored by your request and will probably tell you if he/she cannot do so for whatever reason. Meet with this person at least once a month and more when you need advice or just someone to listen. It is important to have a trusted colleague as your mentor because he/she is trained in your field and has a different perspective than your spouse. Your spouse or friend or family member may be a good listener, but you do not need to share confidential work information with them. These individuals will support and encourage you because they care for you, but you also need a mentor who will tell you the truth and who is experienced in your field.

Do not tell your mentor the names of students or employees when seeking advice. I have several close colleagues who I know I can call on their personal cell phone if I need immediate feedback on a hot issue. They know they can call me as well. We depend on each other to make the best decision possible when there is a doubt. These times will be few, but when you need someone to give you feedback, you need that feedback quickly.

In addition to hot issues, talk to your mentor about your ideas for new programs. Your mentor's advice may help you to avoid mistakes. Be proactive. Before implementing a new idea, discuss it with teachers, parents, and students, and look for its shortcomings before it is out in the public eye.

Also, choose a personal mentor to guide you in moral and ethical decisions. This person should be an individual that you trust and respect. Select a person who loves you and strives to help you to be successful in life. This might be a trusted friend or family member. When I am struggling with a difficult situation, I rely on guidance from my father. It is helpful to have an unbiased opinion during stressful, trying times. I know I can depend on my father's wise advice to guide me in the direction I need to go when faced with challenging situations.

Strive to model excellence in all you do. Be proactive. Seek accountability by being as transparent as possible in your actions. Seek accountability by avoiding potential problems or potholes. Remember—it is easier to avoid potholes than it is to repair your wheel alignment.

Seek guidance when you need it from a trusted mentor. Before implementing a new program, discuss it with key personnel and other stakeholders.

As iron sharpens iron, so one man sharpens another.

—King Solomon, Proverbs 27:17 (NIV)

5

THE PRINCIPAL MODELS CHARACTER EDUCATION

Have you ever heard the phrase "If momma ain't happy, ain't nobody happy"? This saying implies that the mother sets the tone for the household. If the mother is not happy, no one will be happy. There is wisdom and truth in this saying: My mother maintains the most optimistic view of life! She wakes up each morning full of energy and enthusiasm. I truly cannot recall a time that she lounged in her nightgown in the morning. She pops out of bed, gets dressed immediately, and applies her make-up and styles her hair. Then, she heads to the kitchen to get the day started. Usually, she has the radio or television playing in the background. She listens to the popular music; it is upbeat and happy. I find I walk out of the door ready to face the world with an energetic outlook when I leave my parents' house because my mother sets a happy, optimistic tone for the day.

THE PRINCIPAL SETS THE TONE OF THE SCHOOL

And so it is in each school. The principal sets the tone of the school. The principal's philosophy should radiate through each employee in the building. For example, I stress being kind and respectful to others. Therefore, I expect the employees I supervise to put a high priority on treating others with kindness and respect. I communicate this expectation to them. The tone is set by communicating my expectations and modeling this behavior consistently. Character education begins with the principal who sets the tone for the school, just as the mother and father set the tone at home. It will not be what the principal *says* that people will remember; it will be what the principal actually *does* that will be long remembered.

What kind of character will you model? Will you treat others with kindness and respect? Will you talk or gossip about others? Will you smile and speak to others while gently encouraging them through your comments and positive body language? Decide now about the kind of character you want to model for the faculty, staff, students, and parents with whom you work, and change your actions accordingly.

Character is power.

—Booker T. Washington

LIVING THE GOLDEN RULE

Treat others the way you want to be treated.

—The Golden Rule

Most people are familiar with the golden rule, found in a multitude of religions and in the New Testament of the Bible, which states: "So in everything, do to others what you would have them do to you, for this sums up the Law and the Prophets."

My mother and father provided a perfect example of the Golden Rule one evening. After my father announced his candidacy for re-election as mayor of my hometown, he and my mother planned a supper for approximately 175 people who had served in key leadership positions during his first campaign. My parents rented the recreation center to have this celebration. At the end of the dinner and after everyone had left, my family and I cleaned up the tables and leftover food. We were all exhausted; we had all worked that day, and my husband and I had driven from out of town to attend the event. Needless to say, we were ready to leave.

My father thoughtfully called the firemen and invited them to come and take the leftovers to the firehouse. After the firemen left, I was totally focused on getting in the car and going home when my mother announced that we could not leave yet. She said there was a young woman in the building who was responsible for locking the recreation center and we could not leave her alone to do so. After mother made this declaration, she and my father went back into the building and waited for the young woman to turn off the lights and lock the doors. My parents walked her out of the recreation center and into the parking lot, and we all left together.

This was a profound learning experience for me. I realized that I had just learned the best lesson about the golden rule. My parents demonstrated, through their actions, how they would want another person to treat their daughter or how my mother would want to be treated. They stayed with this young woman until the job was finished. Their kindness was truly a living example of the golden rule.

Shoes

I have had a love affair with shoes since I was a little girl. In fact, Aunt Lib, my great aunt, enjoys teasing me about my affection for shoes when I was young. Her favorite story is how I did not like to take my shoes off when I was a child. When I was three or four years old, I would kick and scream if my mother tried to remove my shoes. She grew tired of my kicking and bruising her, so one night she pronounced I could sleep with my shoes on! To this day, Aunt Lib will tease me about this story and will ask me if I still like to sleep with my shoes on my feet. I adore shoes. I am not like Imelda Marcos; I do not have hundreds of shoes in my closet. I do, however, enjoy looking at the new shoe styles as they emerge, and I like to observe shoes as I "people watch" at the local mall.

Jesus was a great storyteller. He was a master teacher who spoke plainly and used simple language to communicate with others. He used parables and metaphors to convey his message. I also like to use stories and metaphors when speaking to others to help get my message across to them. I use *shoes* as a metaphor when speaking to students about the golden rule. Through the years, I have witnessed students being unkind to each other—especially in middle school—so when I have the opportunity, I try to use creative avenues to get students' attention to make them think about their actions and responsibilities.

During one speech, I asked a young woman if I could borrow her shoe. (I asked her for permission before I began my speech in front of hundreds of people.) She willingly obliged. I held her shoe up for the audience to see and I explained that I knew what she was anxious about in making the transition to high school because I have "worn her shoes" so to speak. I have been a student and teacher before becoming a principal, I explained. I encouraged my students to think about each other and the possible struggles they might be facing at home or in the classroom. I admonished them to be kind to each other and treat each other the way they wanted to be treated.

In another speech, I wore two different shoes! I took my shoes off during my speech and used them as a visual aid to discuss free will or freedom of choice. I told the students I chose to wear two different shoes that morning. I further explained that each day we have a multitude of decisions to make. Some decisions are simple—like what to wear each day. Other decisions affect our life in a more serious way. There are numerous decisions that students will make on their own. I encouraged them to talk to their parents and teachers when struggling with a decision and told them to not take any action that they would not be proud to talk about with their parents.

Shoes at the Holocaust Museum

When I visited the Holocaust Museum in Washington, D.C., I developed a new appreciation for shoes. The museum has a floor that houses a display of shoes that were discovered in a concentration camp. The shoes fill a glass room; they are stacked one on the other and fill the display. They are old and new, large and small. They come from men and women and little children. They are the actual shoes of real people who were killed in those terrible concentration camps.

After this visit to the Holocaust Museum, I saw shoes in a new way. Shoes represent people. I think of what it would be like to wear another person's shoes and assume their responsibilities as well as their burdens. Seeing shoes in this new light made me more empathetic. It made me stop and think of others more than I think of myself. Shoes remind me of the golden rule. Shoes remind me to treat others the way I want to be treated. I communicate this message to my students by using shoes as objects to which they can relate.

HOW DO YOU MODEL CHARACTER EDUCATION AT YOUR SCHOOL?

How do you live the golden rule? What lessons do others learn from you as they watch you from afar? How do you treat the adults and students with whom you work each day? Do you practice the golden rule and insist that students and employees treat others like they would want to be treated? I once told my faculty that my expectation was beyond the golden rule. I explained that I wanted them to treat our students like they would want *their* children treated. Remember the principal models character education each day at school.

Don't judge a man until you've walked two moons in his moccasins.

—Native American Saying

6

GIVE CREDIT WHERE DUE
AND PUT A LITTLE LIGHT ON IT

GIVERS AND TAKERS

There are two kinds of people: Givers and Takers. Let's think about some extreme examples of each. *Givers* are the employees who volunteer to sponsor clubs and chaperone events. Givers do extra at work. Even if they cannot help in the evening due to family obligations, Givers are people who you know you can count on in tough times. These are the people who smile and encourage their colleagues and students. They are passionate about their career choices; they love teaching and it shows. Givers think of others and help others through service and encouragement.

Takers, on the other hand, are people who are there for "pay day and quitting time." Takers will not serve on committees or volunteer to help with special projects. They complain about what is wrong with the school or district but will not get involved to improve matters. Takers rarely volunteer in the community. They expect others to keep the world functional for them. Takers think only of themselves.

Which one are you? My guess is that you are a Giver or you would not be a current or future principal. Recognize that there are Givers and Takers among your faculty and staff, and go forward with your vision for your school. You will not change people. It is unlikely that Takers will become Givers overnight—or ever. Focus on the positive vision you have for your school and do not be distracted by the Takers.

> *Givers think of others and help them through their service and encouragement while Takers think only of themselves.*
>
> —Jan Irons Harris

GIVE CREDIT WHERE CREDIT IS DUE

I think I have learned that the best way to lift one's self up is to help someone else.

—Booker T. Washington

During your journey, you will experience successes. You will have opportunities, I hope, to be in the spotlight because of the programs you create, as well as the accomplishments of faculty, staff, and students. When these opportunities arise, share the glory. Acknowledge the contributions of others. Look for genuine ways to give credit where credit is due.

There are a number of general ways in which you give credit where credit is due. When you are accepting an award for the school, you have a public opportunity to recognize the faculty, staff, parents, and students for their involvement. You have an opportunity to thank those who supported the school with their money, time, and talents. You have the chance to thank your supervisor for his/her support.

Give Credit through Formal Letters of Commendation

I like to recognize significant contributions in a formal written manner with a letter of commendation or an email. Letters are powerful tools that are appreciated and treasured. I remember reading such a letter at an athletic banquet one night. The volleyball team won a state championship, and I was invited to their celebration dinner. At the awards portion of the program, I read the letter of commendation I wrote for the coach, Melanie Donahoo. I commended her in the presence of her team and their parents and then placed this letter in her personnel file. Take the opportunity to write commendation letters and present them in public settings when an individual achieves a monumental accomplishment. You will find this method of "giving credit where credit is due" to be effective and appreciated. See appendix B for a sample letter of commendation.

It is rewarding to recognize the accomplishments of students, as well. I remember sending letters to the parents of students who excelled in my classroom while I was teaching mathematics. I sent a commendation letter to Mr. and Mrs. Langston because their son, Russell, had the highest average in my algebra class. I wrote and told them so on official school letterhead. I congratulated Russell for his academic achievement and commended him for consistently being prepared for class and displaying nice manners. Mrs. Langston told me she placed this letter in Russell's baby book. Russell ultimately earned his college degree in mathematics and computer science. Mrs. Langston gives me some of the credit for Russell's major accomplishment because I helped to encourage him along the way.

Remember those people who "made it happen." Recognize those individuals who "do the right thing." Give credit where credit is due. By doing so, you will encourage future leadership and participation. You will build teams and raise morale at your school. You are the leader of the school, but remember—it's not about you. It is about the team members you represent.

Do not withhold good from those who deserve it, when it is in your power to act.

—King Solomon, Proverbs 3:27 (NIV)

PUT A LITTLE LIGHT ON IT

I hope you never have to deal with a scandal, but chances are pretty good that you will have to do so during the time you are in the principal's office. I recall an experience where an employee and his wife were involved in a domestic dispute. She called the local television news and reported that her husband had stolen property from the school and it was in their garage. This news was presented on television, and everyone was talking about it.

The morning after the story ran on the news, I called a team leader meeting in my office. I chose to "put a little light on the matter." We stood for this brief meeting in my office. I held a positive view and reminded them that we are innocent until proven guilty in the United States of America. I told them I believed in our employee and did not believe there was truth in this allegation. I gave them the facts as I knew them. The superintendent had placed the individual on administrative leave until the matter was investigated. It actually went to the grand jury, where the employee was exonerated. Afterward, he returned to work.

During the scandal, I chose to use "light" to maintain a professional atmosphere. Rather than having people standing around whispering about the incident and wondering about it, I chose to "put a little light on it" and tell them what I knew, what I thought, and how I was going to handle this situation. Afterward, everyone went back to work. The scandal was minimized and we focused on our number-one priority: teaching our students.

If you experience a scandal:

- Get the facts from your supervisor. Remember to follow the chain of command.
- Communicate the facts to your faculty and staff without violating the privacy rights of an individual. In the example I shared with you, I never discussed any confidential information with the teachers. I simply gave the facts that I could in order to return the focus to teaching our students.
- Prepare a statement for the media. Be ready to respond if you are asked for a statement.
- Stop talking about it. Move on. Return the focus to the mission of your school.
- Set an example with your behavior.

THE TRUTH

Then you will know the truth, and the truth will set you free.

—John 8:32 (NIV)

Tell the truth. Always tell the truth. When asked a question, answer it honestly. Tell the truth. If you cannot answer the question because of confidentiality, tell the person that you cannot answer due to confidentiality issues. Telling the truth simplifies your life. When you are honest with your supervisor, there are no hidden issues and you develop a relationship built on honesty and trust. If your supervisor asks you a question about an employee or student, answer it honestly and succinctly.

While in the principal's office, you will be like a minister or doctor in that people will share confidences with you. Do not breach this trust unless you have to do so. There are times when this will be necessary but those will be the anomaly. An example of having to breach a trust is when a student threatens to commit suicide. In this case, you have a duty to warn others and must contact a parent immediately.

The Principal Does Not Gossip

Tell the truth, but do not use this admonition as an excuse to gossip about others. There will be cases where others will criticize your supervisor or board members. Do not participate in this dialogue even if it is the truth. Be silent. I have had more than one situation where this actually occurred. In two instances, I recall another person saying, "Jan will not talk about her boss." If a person makes a derogatory comment about someone with whom I work and then says something to me such as "Do you like him/her?" I try to respond with a positive comment or I remain silent. I do not show any sign that I agree with them, then I try to change the subject. Refuse to criticize or gossip about the people with whom you work; strive to make a positive comment about the person mentioned.

Be not curious about the affairs of others . . .

—George Washington, 1745, from George Washington's *Rules of Civility and Decent Behavior in Company and Conversation*

The Principal Tells the Truth

Tell the truth. Tell the truth gently. Tell the truth with respect and humility. If you think a decision your supervisor made is a mistake, tell him or her, but so do privately and respectfully. I once made an appointment with my superintendent and told her I wanted permission to honestly tell her what I thought about a particular matter. She told me to proceed. I explained what I thought and why I felt that way. I explained my fear that this direction might hurt her in the future. I told her I respected her authority and would subject myself to her authority, as always, if she chose to stay with her decision, but that I had to let her know how I felt about this issue. She listened, thanked me for coming, and later changed direction. She appreciated my respect as well as my honesty and courage to tell the truth. Even if she had not agreed with me, I would have felt good about stating my position and being true to myself.

Be known for being transparent. If a teacher asks you for advice, honestly but gently give the advice to the person. If you are reprimanding an individual, do so with kindness and honesty. If you are evaluating an employee, do so honestly and with grace. Tell the truth. This does not mean to bluntly tell the truth in a written evaluation. For example, first try to correct a behavior by talking to an individual about the area that needs improvement before putting this recommendation or directive in a written format.

Truth is the only safe ground to stand upon.

—Elizabeth Cady Stanton

7

TESTS AND EXAMINATIONS

Life in the Fishbowl and Directing Traffic Naked

While you are in the principal's office, you will be tested and examined. This is a natural phenomenon. Understand that this is the way it will probably be for the rest of your life. I have heard others talk about principals in every school in which I have worked—this is life. Human beings like to criticize and complain to each other at times. They also like to gossip. Understand this as you enter the principal's office. Your choices will be thoroughly discussed, choices such as where you choose to live and attend church. I have even heard women talk about where female administrators shop and what size clothes they wear!

This should not be a surprise to you because we are saturated with media coverage of celebrities and criminals. We, in America, seem to be almost obsessed with watching other people. As you enter the principal's office, remember this fact and it will prepare you for the times you will be criticized.

LIFE IN THE FISHBOWL

I keep a small glass fish in a six-inch fishbowl on the shelf in my office bathroom. This poor little fish has no privacy. He "swims" around while people watch. He is a beautiful fish. He doesn't seem to mind. His presence in my bathroom is a source of strength to me. It reminds me that the fish is me! Life in the principal's office is life in the fishbowl. I know that I can handle the truth about life in the principal's office when I look at him and see myself. I remember that I do not mind being watched, studied, criticized, and compared because I understand it is part of the job. I realize, and you should too, that you are living life in the fishbowl. Make your choices accordingly.

With life in the fishbowl, realize that there is no such thing as a private conversation. In one instance, a colleague who served as principal experienced marital problems and shared this confidential information with an employee, who could not keep this newsflash to himself. By sharing it with others, this busybody was able to show that he had power in the school because the principal had shared this private information with him. This news went through the school like a wildfire. People began watching this principal more closely after this titillating revelation.

In another situation, a teacher came to see me one day and wanted to know if she had a chance of being named principal. She did not want others to know she was applying for a vacant principal position if she had no chance of getting the job. With kindness, I told her that if she was not ready to let others know she wanted to be a principal, and if she did not want to bear the embarrassment if she was not selected, then she was not ready to assume the principalship. Possessing a willingness to be "out there" is an important step to becoming a principal.

Remember, you are living life in the fishbowl. There are no curtains in that fishbowl, by the way. It is clear throughout the bowl. Do not be surprised when you find yourself in the fishbowl. You are there, my friend. Look closer. Be smart. Be careful. Remember that other people like to watch the fish swim but do not have the courage to get in the fishbowl. This truth will strengthen you as you realize that only few people possess the inner stamina required of life in the principal's office.

DIRECTING TRAFFIC NAKED

Another analogy I like to use that is related to the transparency required of all principals comes from a personal experience. I remember waking up one Sunday morning to find the front page of my local paper filled with comparisons of local officials' salaries. One of the high school principals was captured in a school photo right there—on the front page! Her age, education, and salary were listed below her name.

I was able to experience this "naked" sensation myself when I was selected as a finalist for the superintendent position in which I currently serve. It was Sunday morning. My husband Wholey retrieved the newspaper, and we began our Sunday ritual of having coffee while reading the paper. There I was on the front page of the paper. The article contained my photo along with my age, education, salary, and experience. When we went to church that morning, a friend asked me what it was like having my personal information on the front page of the paper. I told him it was like directing traffic naked! With a sense of humor, I quipped to my friend that I was glad that the newspaper did not share my weight in the article.

Remember this: There are hoops through which you must jump in order to become a principal. If you are not strong enough to be "out there" directing traffic naked, then maybe this position is not suited to your personality. In the principal's office, there are no secrets—your faculty, staff, and students will watch you and model you. They will also talk about you from time to time. Be aware this is a normal part of life in the fishbowl. You will sometimes have to direct traffic naked.

I realize, and you should, too, that you are living life in the fishbowl.

—Jan Irons Harris

8

BE AN ORIGINAL

We've going now into the world. Let your light so shine and let your joy be so obvious that all who come to know you will praise God.

—Larry Dill

LET YOUR LIGHT SHINE

Our former minister, Dr. Larry Dill, faithfully closed our Sunday worship with the following benediction: "We're going now into the world. Let your light so shine and let your joy be so obvious that all who come to know you will praise God."

I find this benediction to be incredibly inspiring and often repeat it in the morning hours. If you are happy to be the principal of your school, it should be easy to recognize this fact simply by looking at you. At school, do others see you smiling and happy at school or fretful and frustrated? Do you maintain a positive outlook and encourage others to do the same?

JOIE DE VIVRE

One morning before school, a student asked me why I was always so happy. He said he noticed I was always happy—even in the morning! I explained to him that I have, as the French say, the *joie de vivre*. This means the hearty or carefree enjoyment of life. I have joy in my heart and I am not ashamed that I am a happy person. I am joyful because I know the meaning of my life, and I enjoy living life every day. I am fortunate to have a career in an area in which I am passionate. I love working with children of all ages. I have many blessings in my life.

The first day I was in the principal's office, I was intimidated. While sitting at my desk, I thought about how I would be defined in my new position. I thought about the manner in which Mr. Sid Ingram, my previous principal and mentor, had run his school. Should I try to be like him? Mr. Tom Drake, a colleague who had many years of service in the principal's office, called to congratulate me. During our conversation, he reminded me to just be myself. He told me that was what had gotten me to the principal's office. "So don't change a thing," he told me, "just be yourself." I was relieved when I hung up the phone. He was right—and I was reassured. I did not have to try to be like Mr. Ingram or anyone else. I could just be me. In other words, let *my* light shine. That is exactly what I have done through the years. I have been me. I have let *my* light shine.

Now, I encourage you to let your light shine. Do not try to be like anyone else. Be yourself. That is what got you to the principal's office. Let your light shine. You are special; you are unique. You set the tone for your entire school. If you are happy and feel blessed to have been selected to lead your school, act like it and let your light shine!

This Little Light of Mine

This little light of mine, I'm gonna let it shine.
This little light of mine, I'm gonna let it shine.
This little light of mine, I'm gonna let it shine
Let it shine all the time, let it shine!
Hide it under a bushel, no! I'm gonna let it shine.
Hide it under a bushel, no! I'm gonna let it shine.
Hide it under a bushel, no! I'm gonna let it shine.
Let it shine all the time, let it shine!

—*Children's church song derived from an*
African American spiritual

FOLLOW YOUR BLISS

Joseph Campbell said, "When you follow your bliss . . . doors will open . . . where there wouldn't be a door for anyone else" (*The Hero's Journey*, 1990, p. 214). You are a unique person. Be an original. Proudly wear your customized personality and sense of style and leadership. Follow your instincts. Follow your heart. Go where your interests lead you.

What Will You Be Remembered For in Later Years?

What do you want to be remembered for, even years after you leave your school? I want to be remembered for character education, the arts, reading, and technology. I also want to be remembered for my creativity and public-speaking skill. Thus, I work on these areas and dedicate time in and out of the office in order to promote these important areas.

For example, I love music. I listened to classical music as I wrote this chapter. Music inspires and energizes me. When I listen to music, I am following my bliss. When I create a new arts program along with other educators, I am following my bliss. Can you define your bliss? Are you following your bliss?

When you follow your bliss . . . doors will open . . . where there wouldn't be a door for anyone else.

—Joseph Campbell, *The Hero's Journey*

WHEN IN DOUBT—DON'T!

While in the principal's office, you will make numerous decisions. You were selected for this key leadership position because your supervisors trusted your judgment. They consider you a wise individual; otherwise, you would not have been given the keys to your school and access to the finances and total educational program.

When you have a reservation about any matter, do not hesitate to think about the matter overnight. Do not feel rushed to make a decision when you need more time to gather information and to think about the issue. Most decisions will come easily but some will not. Talk to your mentor to seek additional input, if needed. I found it helpful to present ideas and requests to the teacher leaders of the school when making decisions that would affect the entire school. In high school, these teachers were the department heads, and in middle school, we had team leaders. It is also helpful to talk to one or two of the most respected teachers to get their input prior to making a decision that you are questioning.

You can be certain that there will be difficult decisions for you to make on a daily basis. Years ago, when I was struggling with a decision regarding a request I received, I decided that when in doubt, for whatever reason, I would not approve the request. Examples where you might be in doubt of whether something is appropriate include a teacher seeking permission to take the students on a field trip or students seeking permission to conduct a new event at the school.

This approach of saying no when in doubt has worked well for me through the years. It is not always easy, but I find that my moral compass is a good guide for me, and your compass will be as well. Trust your inner voice. By simply being yourself, you have attained the honor of serving as a role model and leader at your school. Your opinion counts. Your reservations count. Be conservative. Trust your instincts.

When in doubt—don't!

—Jan Irons Harris

SUMMARY OF PART I

Keys for Spiritual Balance

1. Define your mission, foundation, values, goals, and beliefs. Together, these important parts of your spiritual being form your internal glue. They strengthen you and keep you together in times of stress and examinations.
2. Renew and refine each day. You will strengthen your internal glue by seeking continual growth and improvement in all areas of your life.
3. Separate your personal values and beliefs from the values and principles that govern our country. Understand and separate "church and state." Do not let your beliefs influence your decisions when you know your belief is in direct opposition to the law.
4. Live a proactive life in the principal's office. Avoid potholes by identifying them and through accountability. Seek further accountability through guidance from a trusted mentor.
5. Model your beliefs daily. The principal serves as a model for character education in and out of the principal's office.
6. Help others by encouraging them and guiding them through difficult situations. Encourage others by giving them credit when credit is due. Defuse situations by putting a little light on them: Instead of whispering about newsflashes, employees will know the true story and return to the focus of the school—teaching our students.
7. Understand that you are the fish in the fishbowl. People are watching you. Acknowledging this truth will strengthen you as you "direct traffic naked."
8. Be you! Proudly stand as an original. Trust your instincts in all you do. You are a respected individual. You have been given the keys to your building and responsibility for the entire program at your school. Boldly display your personality through your attitude and actions on a daily basis.

II

PHYSICAL BALANCE

The physical domain is essential in order to maintain optimal health and fitness. Sleep, play, exercise, proper diet, posture, grooming, and manners are a few elements of this domain. Ignoring this important area in your life is like forgetting to put gasoline in your car before going on a trip. We do ourselves a grave injustice if we deny ourselves the right to perform at the highest physical level possible. For, what will our accomplishments matter if we die at an early age due to a stress-related illness or an illness attained through improper diet and lack of exercise?

The sum of the whole is this: walk and be happy; walk and be healthy.
The best way to lengthen out our days is to walk steadily and with a purpose.

—Dickens in *Dictionary of Thoughts* (1877)

9

BODY MAINTENANCE

Rest, Play, and Exercise

PHYSICAL BALANCE—WHAT DOES IT MEAN?

While you are in the principal's office, you will be stretched in a plethora of directions. You will have events to supervise in the evenings and after school. You will have community events in which you will be expected to participate. You will continue to have family and home responsibilities. In spite of the heavy demands placed on you while you serve in the principal's office, you must take care of yourself. No one else will do this for you. It is easy to cut corners where your personal health is involved in order to meet the daily demands of a principal, but do not do this. Take care of yourself to ensure that you are in optimal physical condition.

When I was a high school principal, a faculty member came to visit me one afternoon after school. During our conversation, she told me that she noticed my car in the school parking lot frequently after hours and on the weekends when she passed by the school. She was an educator with years of experience and was close to retirement. This colleague had worked with several principals during her career. Because she cared about me, she took time to share a few of her observations. In particular, she remembered a principal who arrived in the principal's office as a young, energetic man. She sadly noted that when he left the principal's office he was old—not in actual years, but in a depleted, worn-out manner due to the high stress level of the job. We talked about our U.S. presidents and how they seem to age at a fast rate while they are serving as president. Stress can certainly age a person, we agreed.

This veteran educator cautioned me to take care of myself and advised me to not work too many hours. She warned me that serving in the principal's office can extract a lot from your life if you let it. I appreciated this thoughtful friend and colleague taking time to share this important warning with me. Through the years, I have remembered her advice and tried to make it a priority to take care of myself.

TAKE CARE OF YOUR BODY

You have one life to live, so cherish your body and maximize your health and well-being. Take care of the body God gave you. Eat right—especially breakfast! Avoid smoking and being around smoke. Limit or eliminate alcohol. Take a conservative approach to consuming over-the-counter medications and prescription drugs. Listen to your doctor.

See a Family Doctor, Have an Annual Physical, See a Dentist

Speaking of doctors, make sure you get a family doctor; develop a relationship with him or her. Through the years, you can be comforted knowing you have a doctor that cares about you on a personal basis. Have an annual physical and know that you are healthier by having regular check-ups and exams, such as a mammogram (women) or an annual check of your prostrate-specific antigen (PSA) level (men). Also, take care of your teeth while at work and at home. Go to the dentist every six months and keep an extra toothbrush and dental floss at your office.

Rest, Exercise, Eat Healthy Foods

Be sure to get the rest your fine-tuned body requires. Listen to your body. Exercise regularly. Participate in weight-bearing activities in order to ward off osteoporosis and muscle loss as you age. Stretch often. Breathe. Eat proper, nutritious meals and do not fall victim to consuming excessive fast food due to the demands on your time each day. Make healthy eating a priority in your life, and take a multivitamin.

Wash Your Hands!

Wash your hands frequently (this is especially important while working with children!). Keep a bottle of hand sanitizer in your car and also at your desk and use it frequently. Wipe phones and door handles with handy disinfectant wipes or cloths moistened with water and a small amount of Clorox.

Wear Sunscreen

Respect the sun and protect your skin from its damaging rays. You will be supervising students outdoors as they arrive and depart each day. Additionally, you will be attending ballgames and other events outside. Apply sunscreen each day on your face, ears, and hands. Wear a hat when you are out in the sun. You will appreciate this in later years when you avoid skin cancer.

Be Well-Groomed

Take care of your grooming needs. Maintain a regular appointment for haircuts. Have your clothes altered so that they fit you properly. Select your clothes for the next day prior to retiring for the night; lay them out or hang them on a hook on the outside of your closet door. Purchase a steamer to use regularly so that your clothes will be freshly pressed each day. Simplify your wardrobe by minimizing the number of colors and styles that fit your body shape and skin tone. Keep your shoes shined and in good repair. Read chapter 11 for more tips on grooming.

Take Care of Yourself

Be sure to take good care of yourself every day. No one else will take care of you. You are charged with this responsibility. You must be intrinsically motivated to make maintaining your health a daily part of your normal routine. You must respect your body by your own volition. Your self-discipline or lack of self-discipline is mirrored through your body. Your daily choices of food, beverage, exercise, and presentation are testimonials to your self-discipline and philosophy of life.

> . . . *honor God with your body.*

> —Apostle Paul, 1 Corinthians 6:20 (NIV)

REST AND SLEEP

Rest, play, and exercise are important elements in your overall physical well-being. You need times of rest just as a child needs to nap after extended play. You need a good night's sleep every single night. You cannot afford to have a bad day due to lack of sleep. Sleep and rest are tools that will help you to perform at your peak level. Brief periods of rest, taken during the day or before an evening of responsibility, will provide rejuvenation and refreshment.

On busy days that preface a night of supervision, go home for an hour or two to relax after school is out. Some people, including me, find that a thirty-minute nap will provide sufficient rejuvenation needed to be fresh for an evening of activities. After arising from a short nap, take a brisk shower to fully restore yourself. If you cannot go home for an hour or so, at a minimum, get away from your office for a few minutes to refresh. Go for a walk or drive to one of your favorite restaurants and purchase a favorite healthy treat such a mocha milkshake or strawberry-banana smoothie to energize you. Or stop for a moment and have a cup of coffee in order to take a break.

During the week and on the weekend, my grandparents religiously took a well-deserved nap after enjoying a big midday meal. They knew how to relax and enjoy the slower pace of a Sunday afternoon in the country. They rested. By the way, my grandparents did not feel guilty about taking a nap. Instead, it was expected, deserved, and eagerly anticipated. After napping, they continued to relax and enjoy the day by visiting with family and friends.

Sufficient Sleep

Early to bed and early to rise makes a man healthy, wealthy and wise.

—Benjamin Franklin

Benjamin Franklin was right. Going to bed early does make a positive difference in one's performance. Teachers recognize this truth. They encourage students to go to bed early each night because they know that students perform at a higher academic level when they are rested. Principals also need sufficient rest each night. If you are a high school principal, it will be difficult to consistently go to bed early due to meetings and the myriad sports activities each night at your school. But when you have the opportunity, go to bed early.

When you go to bed early, the added benefit is that you are ready to get up early the next morning. You can also find extra time early in the morning when you plan ahead. In order to make your morning less stressful, try to do as much as you can before going to bed. Select clothes for the next day; straighten your house. Charge your cell phone and/or Blackberry. Put your keys and wallet or purse, along with your briefcase or laptop computer, near the door. If you enjoy coffee, purchase a coffee pot that has an automatic timer so you can make it the night before. It is wonderful to awaken in the morning to the smell of coffee brewing.

An "early to bed, early to rise" way of life allows the practitioner to have beneficial time to think, pray, study, or exercise. Because my parents employ this discipline, they walk a couple of miles each day at 6:00 a.m. My mother records the number of miles they walk each day on her calendar; she tallies the number of miles walked at the conclusion of the year. This year they walked 500 miles! With a busy schedule, it is necessary to use each minute of the day to its maximum benefit. You can accomplish monumental tasks, it seems, when you are able to capture extra early morning hours.

Sufficient sleep is needed on a daily basis. Each person requires a different amount of sleep even though most people require between six and eight hours of sleep each night. If I do not set an alarm, I will naturally awaken after eight to eight-and-a-half hours of sleep. This means that in order for me to arise at 5:30 a.m., I need to go to bed at 9:00 p.m. so I can get the proper amount of sleep needed for my body. How much sleep do you naturally require? When you are sleep-deprived, catch up on your lost sleep on the weekend by sleeping late, by going to bed early one night, or by indulging in an extended nap on Sunday afternoon.

Make Your Bedroom a Haven for Rest and Relaxation

To promote tranquil slumber, make your bedroom a haven for rest and relaxation. Do not keep work items in your bedroom. Instead, keep your bedroom free from stress by simplifying its contents and keeping it in order. Make sure you have sufficient light above or beside your bed so you can read in bed before falling off to sleep. For pure enjoyment, keep current magazines along with a favorite book beside the bed for easy access. Keep a radio, CD player, or MP3 player nearby so you can listen to music as another option to relax prior to falling asleep.

Make your bedroom a special environment in which you can feel peacefully comforted. Paint the walls a favorite, quiet color such as khaki, sage, ivory, or soft blue. Treat yourself to nice bed linens. Monogram your sheets and pillowcases and feel special when you recline upon these fresh, clean sheets at night. Sleep under a plush, down comforter or an attractive coverlet. Replace your pillows when needed. Surround yourself with beauty. Arrange your favorite photo, print, or painting so that you can see it when you open your eyes each morning. Clean, dust, and vacuum your bedroom regularly; eliminate clutter. Keep one surface clear so that you can lay items upon it. There is nothing worse than having every inch of space covered with items so that you have nowhere to lay a purse, book, watch, or jewelry when you need to do so.

Sleep Inhibitors

Some people struggle with getting a good night's sleep due to physical ailments. Talk to your doctor if this applies to you. Others struggle with attaining a peaceful sleep due to stress or emotional issues. I am fortunate to be a good sleeper. It is the anomaly if I do not sleep well. I served in the principal's office for more than sixteen years. During this time, there were challenges. There were times that I had to make difficult decisions based on the best interests of my school. The hardest decisions I had to make involved recommending the termination of an employee or expulsion of a student. These serious decisions kept me awake at times. However, I am thankful I am able to sleep well at night most of the time.

You can create the most tranquil bedroom on the planet, but you will not be able to sleep with worry and turmoil in your head. Worry and turmoil are not good bedfellows. We all sleep better at night when we have a clear conscience. When you consistently treat your students and employees fairly, you will not toss and turn at night worrying about the decisions you made. Through the years, I have had parents ask me to please bend the rules for their children. I explain to them I cannot do so because I have to be fair to all of my students; I could not sleep if I gave preferential treatment to students. I predict that you will also have parents who will ask you to relax the rules. Even so, remember to treat students the same way whether they live in a million-dollar home or in a housing project. Be fair and consistent throughout your career.

Defining your mission, values and beliefs (see chapter 1 for more on this) will guide you when faced with the difficult decisions that will be placed on your shoulders. Yes, making a recommendation to terminate an employee will keep me awake at night. However, I realize, and you will too, that when given the decision to recommend someone's termination, principals are faced with two choices: support the employee or support the students. For me, it has been crystal clear that I will support the students because the principal is the protector of children. I am empathetic with the employee's circumstances; however, I believe that our students deserve a competent teacher who is effective in the classroom. Therefore, I make my decisions based on the best interests of my students. I work to improve the teacher's performance and if this is not successful over a reasonable period of time, I have to consider terminating the employee.

What Is on Your Pillow at Night?

When you define your mission, values, and beliefs, you will then have strong internal glue. You will be equipped to face challenges with wisdom and determination. Do the right thing each day. Remember that you will have to place your actions on your pillow each night. Act wisely. Situations will come and go. Students will come and go. You are constantly building your reputation and teaching others about character and integrity through your actions. Display consistency while applying the rules. Be true to yourself. In doing so, you will be postured to sleep like a baby at night because you have a clear conscience. You will awaken refreshed each morning, ready to face a new day filled with new challenges as you work in the principal's office.

Labour to keep alive in your breast that little celestial fire called conscience.

—George Washington, 1745

Tips for Sleeping Like a Baby

- Keep a notepad and pencil on your bedside table within easy reach, so that you can quickly capture any task that needs to be done or record any new ideas. This will remove the thought from your mind and will give you more peace, which will help you to sleep.
- Sleep in total darkness.
- If you own an illuminated digital clock, move it to an angle that will prevent you from seeing it easily if you awaken during the night.
- Avoid caffeine in the evening.
- Sleep in your favorite pajamas. Do not save gift pajamas for special purposes. Enjoy every gift you receive. For men, I suggest to use old, favorite sweaters and jackets that you no longer wear as robes with your pajama bottoms. Women, use your pretty and soft nightgowns that make you happy and comfortable. I keep a white 100 percent cotton nightgown starched and ironed hanging on my bathroom door. It reminds me to look forward to relaxation and peaceful sleep.
- Purchase loungewear for home. Do not look frumpy or sloppy at home! You are in the presence of your family members—the people you love the most in the world! Give them your best presentation. Invest in a couple of comfortable outfits to lounge in on Sunday afternoon. One of my favorite lounge

outfits is black yoga pants and a school t-shirt. I also keep a white cotton zip-up hooded sweatshirt to wear over any outfit. White matches everything.

- Purchase the best house shoes you can find. Your feet deserve it! My husband wears a pair of Merrill clogs inside the house only; he never wears these shoes outside. My favorite indoor shoes are the fur-lined Crocs clogs. I also love to wear simple ballet shoes that I've lined with a foot cushion to make them softer. My favorite socks to wear at home are made by Peds because they are thin and soft.

- Get with the season! During the holidays, have fun by wearing pajamas that are in tune with the holiday. This morning I had on a long "I love New York" t-shirt over white leggings, my white, hooded zip-up sweatshirt, and a Santa hat! My husband laughed when he saw me with the Santa hat. I like to make my family smile and laugh when I am with them.

- Control your thoughts. Compartmentalize issues. For example, around 8:30 p.m., I try to stop thinking about any topic related to work and start thinking about beautiful thoughts. I think about my areas of interests. I read books for enjoyment. I call this "frivolous reading." Do not get in bed and start thinking about negative thoughts. My friend said she struggled with this because, when she gets in bed, "the committee convenes." She said she starts replaying issues that occurred in the past or worries about future events. Do not do this! You have dominion over your mind. Control your thoughts. Tell yourself that you are not thinking about this thought now.

- If you cannot sleep, train your mind to go to the most peaceful, beautiful memory you have stored in your personal computer (your brain). For me, a lovely remembrance is related to a vacation we had in Hawaii. I remember the warmth of the sun upon me as I stretched beneath it on Waikiki beach. I had no worries. I was soaking in the sun and I remember thinking that the Pacific Ocean was absolutely exquisite. The water was crystal clear and the sky was unusually blue that day. I was twenty-seven years old at the time and this remains a vivid memory. What is a special, happy memory for you? Use this memory to help you unwind and sleep like a baby.

> . . . whatever is true, whatever is noble, whatever is right, whatever is pure, whatever is lovely, whatever is admirable—if anything is excellent or praise-worthy—think about such things.

> —Apostle Paul, Philippians 4:8 (NIV)

PLAY AND EXERCISE

When is the last time you played ball or went to the park to feed the ducks? When is the last time you played a game of checkers? When is the last time you read a book to a child or had a tea party? Play is an important part of our lives. We miss out when we forget to participate in the simple pleasure of play.

Play does not have to be complicated. My favorite memories of childhood include times when we, as children, were bored and went outside and created our own activity for entertainment. We might start a game of kickball or choose to ride bicycles with our friends while carrying dolls in the front basket of our bicycles. We might decide to form a parade, marching up and down the streets under our umbrellas on sunny days. Whatever activity we chose, we enjoyed it. We played and laughed because they go hand in hand.

In our family, one of our favorite play activities is to throw a ball in the pool, at the beach or in the yard. People of all ages can enjoy this simple activity. Take time to play and laugh each day. When is the last time you played for sheer pleasure?

Model a Healthy Lifestyle

While in the principal's office, make time for play at school and at home. When you are observing physical education classes, get involved occasionally by throwing the ball or even wearing gym clothes one day and sharing a day in the gym with your students to show them you believe in exercise and lifelong wellness activities.

With the rise in obesity over the last few years, we must strive to model healthy lifestyles for our students. Encourage your students to choose a lifelong sport to enjoy. Talk to your students about your interest in tennis, biking, running, walking, or whatever your favorite activity may be. By talking about your personal interest in exercise, others will be encouraged and inspired to also get active.

Lack of Exercise Will Age You

Lack of exercise will age you quickly. You will have a number of meetings each day that will require you to be seated. You will observe classes that will require you to be seated. Look for ways to increase your physical activity. Go up and down staircases instead of riding elevators. Park a little farther out in the parking lot so you can walk and stretch. I like to think that there are people who truly need the front parking spaces, so I pass on these spots—I know I need the exercise anyway. Instead of sending emails to communicate messages, deliver them in person. For example, instead of emailing the coach about a matter, walk down to the gym and talk to him or her about it. By engaging in this physical activity, you will accomplish three goals: you will observe the class, you will monitor the halls on the way en route to the gym, and you will get the extra physical activity you need.

Take Ten

While the suggested activities mentioned above will help you remain active, you must seek a more intensive level of exercise to sustain your health and overall well-being. Check with your doctor before beginning any new exercise program.

While I was in the principal's office, I struggled with finding the time to exercise. I never could seem to schedule a conventional exercise class for a number of reasons. First, I found that in a public class, I became distracted by interacting with people in the class who wanted to exchange information about their student or situation. Second, it was difficult to get to a class after school, go home and shower, and then attend an evening event. If I did not have an event to attend at night, I wanted to be at home to cook supper or go out to eat with my husband. It seemed I was always conflicted in this area.

Finally, I came to the conclusion that I may not have time to attend an exercise class three times a week, but I certainly had ten minutes to do some form of exercise in the morning and in the afternoon. Therefore, I started dedicating ten minutes each morning on my NordicTrack. After I finished the time on the Nordic-Track, I did ten exercises for each part of my body. I did ten stretches upward and then ten stretches downward and ten stretches outward. I did push-ups, sit-ups, and squats. I lifted weights also in this manner. This routine took me approximately twenty minutes, and I was able to do it early in the morning. I recorded the workout on my calendar as a source of encouragement.

In the afternoon, I found I could easily insert twenty minutes of walking into my daily routine. I left a good pair of walking shoes in my office. After school, I would walk around the campus and into the neighborhood. This was simple and it worked for me.

Find a routine that works for you. Do not be discouraged if you cannot find an organized class in which to exercise. Create your own routine and stick to it. You will be more energized and feel less stressed due to the release of endorphins during exercise. Take ten minutes when you need to rejuvenate. Take ten minutes to walk around the campus. Take ten minutes to exercise in the morning. Take ten minutes to walk in the afternoon. All of these ten minutes will add up to a healthier lifestyle. You will be the beneficiary of this investment of ten minutes. Remember that ten minutes are better than zero minutes of physical exercise. What are you waiting for? Take ten!

PHYSICAL FUEL

Food and Water

Those who think they have no time for healthy eating will sooner or later have to find time for illness.

—Edward Stanley, *The Conduct of Life*

I found healthy eating to be a challenge while I was in the principal's office. It seemed there was always a sweet soul who would graciously bring donuts or other goodies to the office for our hard-working staff to enjoy. From time to time, the lunchroom ladies would bake sweet rolls for the faculty and staff to enjoy. I could not resist enjoying these warm-from-the-oven, special treats. Even if I had already eaten breakfast, I still enjoyed these wonderful yeast rolls.

FOOD IS COMFORT

Food is comfort; food is love. I do not know a single person who does not enjoy food. Food can be addictive. One of my friends, unfortunately, went through a terrible divorce; during this ordeal, she turned to food for comfort and ultimately gained a lot of weight. A psychologist helped her recover from this emotional and physical injury. From her negative experience, I learned that we should be cognizant of when we eat and why we eat. Eat only when you are hungry. Do not eat to feel better because of a stressful day, for example. Principals go to meetings where there is often food available. Food is everywhere. In recent years, food can be found even in church on Sunday mornings for people to enjoy prior to the worship service.

THINK ABOUT WHAT YOU EAT, WHY YOU EAT, AND HOW MUCH YOU EAT

Americans are given ample opportunities to overeat. It is ridiculous to see the portions presented to us in restaurants. A single restaurant plate provides enough food to feed my husband and me. However, when we eat out, I notice that he will eat the portion brought to him. We have super-sized drinks and meals at most fast food stores. Only accept food and beverages when you are hungry and think about what you eat, why you eat, and how much you eat. When I am trying to drop a few pounds, I record each item I eat or drink in my journal at the end of each day. This action makes me accountable by forcing me to realize what I have eaten during the day. Socrates said, "Moderation in everything." This is my mantra. I strive to remember the advice of Socrates at all times. An occasional donut will not be damaging. However, a donut each day is not a healthy or wise eating choice.

STRATEGIES FOR HEALTHY EATING

He that takes medicine and neglects diet, wastes the skill of the physician.

—Chinese proverb

Through the years, I have adopted a few strategies that have assisted me in my quest for healthy eating. I purchased a nice Thermos to hold coffee or hot tea. This gives me a good alternative to soft drinks. I also purchased a Thermos to hold hot soup or oatmeal. Surprisingly, hot soup in a Thermos is a delicious and light choice for lunch. I keep a drawer filled with healthy food choices in times of emergencies. Provide good choices for yourself just as you would for one of your students or your own children. I will often prepare a peanut butter sandwich for an afternoon snack if I know I have a long day before me. Select healthy snack choices for extra energy during the day. My favorite snacks include:

- Small can of tuna packed in water
- Individual servings of applesauce
- Small box of raisins
- A handful of almonds
- Trail mix
- Peanut butter crackers
- Canned grapefruit juice or V8™

At any given time, you might find any of these healthy snacks in my desk drawer. I also keep bottled water in my closet along with a box of green tea bags, a coffee cup, a set of flatware, and a travel salt and pepper. These items make my day go better because I am able to replenish my energy reservoir during busy times. I also like to keep individually wrapped peppermints and chocolates in my desk. The peppermint serves as a stimulant during a low energy moment in the afternoon; chocolate is medicinal in moderation and can soothe nerves in times of stress. These items provide comfort and energy. Plan for busy times and stock a drawer with your favorite, healthy choices. By planning, you will reduce the need to snack with unhealthy food choices.

Breakfast and Lunch: Physical Fuel

Here are three recommendations related to breakfast and lunch.

1. Do not EVER skip breakfast!   Breakfast is the most important meal of the day. It gives you the solid energy base you need for a busy, productive work life. Eating breakfast will not only give you energy—it will curb your appetite during the day and your memory will be boosted. An elaborate breakfast is not required but you must take the time to have a decent breakfast, even if it is just a glass of juice and a bagel. I like to keep foods that are easy and quick to eat for breakfast. Some of my quick breakfast items include grapes, cheese slices that are individually wrapped, almonds, chicken, breakfast bars, peanut butter, and juice. When I have more time for breakfast, I enjoy a scrambled egg sandwich; oatmeal with raisins, brown sugar, and almonds; or a toasted bagel with cream cheese.

2. Make time to eat lunch at school.   During my first year as a middle school principal, I recall a time when I met my husband for supper. I told him I was absolutely starving! When he asked me why was I so hungry I explained that I did not have time to eat lunch that day. He told me that this was ridiculous because I was the boss and that I should be able to manage my time so that I have at least fifteen minutes to eat. His practical advice made a huge impact on my time management. After that conversation, I decided I would make time for lunch each day.

I initiated a new lunch routine that allowed me to have time to eat lunch with the custodians before the lunch period began. I invited the assistant principal to join me. It was relaxing to eat lunch before all the students entered the lunchroom because in middle school, lunch is a hectic situation where the adults referee events, such as who took whose potato chips. Additionally, students forget lunch money and there are always issues to resolve in the lunchroom. There is no time to relax in the lunchroom for those on duty, so it is important to schedule time to eat lunch in a relaxed atmosphere before students arrive.

3. Make good, healthy choices for lunch.   With today's improved emphasis on wellness because of the national obesity issue, lunches are much healthier than they were twenty years ago. In fact, I am unaware of any food item in the cafeteria that is fried; even the French fries are baked. The school cafeteria will provide a variety of good, fresh choices for you. Whether you choose to eat the cafeteria food or bring your own lunch from home, eat healthy foods. Eat sweets sparingly. You will feel better and have more energy in the afternoon if you make this positive choice.

I like a variety of choices, so I oscillate between packed lunches and school lunches. A typical packed lunch for me is a ham sandwich with mustard (hold the mayo—it is loaded with calories) on wheat bread, baked chips, raisins or a banana, and a cookie. I also enjoy a small can of tuna or a small yogurt with crackers for lunch.

Banquets

When you enter the principal's office, you automatically assume the responsibility to acknowledge and applaud your students' accomplishments at annual banquets and award ceremonies. At banquets, I found the most popular menu to be chicken, potatoes, green beans, salad, rolls, and dessert. Regardless of the menu, often the choices at banquets are not the healthiest ones. Carefully choose healthy food items at these banquets. Avoid starches, sweets, and fried foods. Instead, select a salad and use dressing sparingly, and choose fresh vegetables. If you enjoy sweets, eat small portions of these items that are void of nutrients and protein. Drink water with your meals instead of sweetened iced tea or sugary soft drinks. Avoid caffeine at these banquets so that you can sleep well later that night.

During the time you are in the principal's office, you will attend a multitude of banquets. Be prepared in advance to be tempted with food choices that may not be part of your quest for a healthy diet. Be disciplined with your food choices at banquets. Do not complain about your choices; simply eat small portions of food in order to be polite, or only select food items, if you are enjoying a buffet, that are in concert with your health goals. If the banquet is a sit-down meal where a prepared plate is presented to you, do not feel that you have to eat everything on your plate. For example, when I received a fried-chicken boxed dinner at a banquet, I removed the skin from the chicken and ate the meat. I avoided the bread and fries, and instead, enjoyed the coleslaw and baked beans. Be a gracious guest and enjoy the celebrations you will be invited to attend. I hope you have many successes to celebrate!

Junk Food

This is a good time to talk about making good choices in general. While in the principal's office, you will be attending numerous meetings and celebrations. Do not fall into the trap of eating junk food at all of these events. If fresh fruit or vegetables are available at these events, this is your best choice. It seems that people are more conscious of making better food choices in America, in general, because of the fact that more than two-thirds of Americans are obese. Because of this epidemic, I hope you will find fewer temptations while you are in the principal's office, but this is probably not going to be the case.

Birthdays and Cupcakes

In Alabama, we are required to have a wellness policy in each school district in the state. Therefore, unhealthy foods are restricted from the schools. For example, soft drinks are totally banned for elementary students. However, as long as children have birthdays, parents will bring cupcakes to celebrate these joyous occasions! Additionally, teachers and parents search for ways to celebrate their students' achievements, and this is often done with food treats. This can be a temptation for you, as principal, if you are constantly eating at these celebrations. Be prepared for food temptations and avoid them when you can. It should be the anomaly when you indulge in a slice of birthday cake or a pastry.

Again, do not forget to eat a healthy breakfast each morning so that you do not start the day being hungry. If you are satisfied, you will be less tempted to take that slice of cake or brownie that the office cook prepared for everyone's enjoyment. There is always one sweet person in the office that enjoys cooking and assuming the role of nurturer. This person will kindly bring delicious unscheduled treats that can sabotage the most disciplined person's diet efforts. Be prepared for the occasional treat. Delayed gratification can assist you when this phenomenon occurs. Take the peanut butter brownie but save it for dessert after lunch, for example. Also, be mindful of portion size and select a small brownie. Do not feel obligated to participate in each celebration by eating at each event. Instead, have water, black coffee, or punch.

In closing, if you indulge in all the special celebrations at your school with food, you will most likely start to gain weight while you are in the principal's office and, at the least, you will be unhealthy. Be prepared and think about creative ways to enjoy these special opportunities with moderation while modeling a disciplined, healthy diet.

Water

Drinking sufficient water keeps you properly hydrated and helps with digestion. An added benefit of staying hydrated is that you will not feel hungry and tempted to snack. Stay hydrated by drinking at least six to eight glasses of water each day. At a minimum, start each morning with a glass of water. Then drink another glass of water during the midmorning and another at lunch. Drink another glass of water in the afternoon and a glass of water with supper. When you walk by a water fountain, take a few sips of water. Keep water accessible in your office. Bring ice water to your office in an insulated cup or bottle and enjoy it throughout the day. Also, keep a clean cup—or disposable cups (if you must)—handy in order to go to the lunchroom to get a cup of ice occasionally. Fill the cup with water and enjoy a refreshing treat of ice water.

Soft Drinks

Strive to avoid soft drinks. I know one teacher who simply eliminated soft drinks from his diet and lost more than thirty pounds by doing so. Calorie-filled, carbonated beverages have the propensity to add pounds to your body and serve as a deterrent for water and juice. If you must have the taste of something besides water, choose a diet, caffeine-free soft drink.

Coffee and Tea

Beverages, like food, comfort us. In the mornings, I enjoy having approximately two cups of caffeinated coffee. The caffeine in the coffee gives me a little boost in the morning to get my day started. I faithfully practice the morning ritual of having one cup of coffee with my husband before he leaves for work. Then, when I arrive in my office, I usually retrieve a cup of coffee before starting my morning work. Some people avoid caffeine at all costs. I mostly like to feel the warmth of the mug in my hand while enjoying the aroma of coffee. I know a principal, Jayne Barnett, who, along with Verna Hale, the school counselor, enjoys an afternoon tea ritual. After the students leave school, these two ladies enjoy a cup of hot tea while they review the day's events and plan for the next day. I do not religiously practice this ritual but I do enjoy it from time to time. If you enjoy coffee or tea, drinking it black will ensure that you do not intake additional calories. Be watchful of calorie-laden trendy coffee and tea specialty beverages.

To eat is a necessity, but to eat intelligently is an art.

—La Rochefoucauld

⓫

PRESENTATION

Grooming, Posture, Confidence, Clothes, Accessories, and Shoes

Keep your nails clean and short, also your hands and teeth clean, yet without showing any great concern for them.

—George Washington, 1745

First impressions are lasting. People form an opinion of you during the first few seconds that they see you. Like it or not—an opinion is formed because of your physical presentation. Your physical presentation includes grooming (is your hair clean and combed?), posture (do you stand tall and proud?), confidence (do you make eye contact with those you meet?), clothes (are your clothes wrinkled and soiled?), accessories (do you have too many accessories that are distracting, such as wearing rings on every finger?), and shoes (are your shoes polished and in good repair?).

GROOMING

Grooming is an essential part of our being; we teach its importance to our children. Daily cleanliness is important for one's health and social acceptance. Different cultures have different grooming expectations. For example, in America, daily showering is a basic expectation for individuals. Additionally, we are expected to have clean, attractively styled hair. Professionals, such as principals, are also expected to have clean, manicured nails and to be dressed in a dignified manner that sets a good example for the teachers and students.

Mr. Ingram, former principal of Grissom High School, was the epitome of a well-dressed principal who consistently modeled exceptional grooming. His hair

Figure 11.1. "Photograph of Mr. Sid Ingram"

was always trimmed and perfectly combed. He was clean-shaven; his smile displayed sparkling, clean teeth. His nails were trimmed and clean. He looked well rested and fresh in the mornings.

Grooming: Specific Tips for Women

Women have supplemental grooming needs. Women usually wear make-up and have more choices to make regarding grooming. The following grooming recommendations are for women:

Hairstyles should be simple, attractive, and not distracting. When parents meet with the principal, they need to focus on the issue being discussed and not be distracted with a bizarre hair style that demands attention. Hair should not be excessively teased. If you color your hair, choose a natural color for your skin tone. Hair should be cut in a style that is easy to manage. I like to wash, dry, and style my hair in the morning and not touch it again the rest of the day. It is worth investing extra money to have the best hairdresser you can find. If you do not have a good hairstylist, when you see someone with an attractive haircut, ask the person who styles her hair. Once you find the right hair stylist for you, keep regular appointments that allow for trimmings. If you go a little sooner for trims than the recommended six-week interval, your hair will consistently look good.

Hair products can help you immensely when managing your hair. My niece, Emily Anderton, is the captain of the dance team at the University of North Alabama. The more than twenty-five girls on the squad have picture-perfect hair. When they perform at football games during halftime, their long, curly hair never moves. One of the products they faithfully use is Freeze It hairspray. In fact, when Emily met with the newly selected dancers, she gave each of them a travel size bottle of the hairspray, telling them to meet their "new best friend." It is a firm hairspray that keeps your hair in place for hours. Emily recommends that the girls use mousse after washing their hair. Additionally, she encourages them to use hair spray gel. An abundance of hair products are available that can help you manage your hair so that this task will become effortless.

Nails should be clean and trimmed. Artificial, long nails painted in a bright red color are distracting in the office setting. Further, these artificial, long nails leave one wondering how the principal works with those long fingernails. Maintain manicured nails that are relatively short and buffed or polished with a natural color. There are numerous clear or neutral colors to choose from at your local drugstore.

Make-up should look natural and not be overpowering. Extreme eye liner or eye shadow can be perceived as being "over the top" at school. During the day, wear less make-up for the office. It is appropriate to wear more make-up for special events in the evening. Remember your professional role during the day and groom for it.

Lipstick is a fundamental grooming element for the professional woman. Enlist the assistance of a specialist to help you select an attractive lipstick that complements your skin tone. Please be sensitive to the color of your clothes when selecting your lipstick of the day. You do not want to wear red lipstick with an orange sweater, for example. Choose colors for lipstick that blend with multiple colors without clashing. Using a lip liner will make your color endure longer. After applying lipstick, try covering your lipstick with a lip gloss or Vaseline™. Again, do not overdo it. A nice lipstick finishes your overall grooming efforts. Keep extra lipstick in your bathroom, desk drawer, and purse to touch up when needed.

Fragrance

Men and women should not wear strong aftershave lotion or perfume to the office. There is nothing worse than being subjected to someone else's sense of what smells good. Perfume should never precede you into a room or linger after you have exited. Additionally, some students and adults have allergies that can be aggravated by intense perfume.

POSTURE

Did you ever watch the Princess of Wales on television? Princess Diana had the most exceptional posture and overall appearance, whether she was visiting patients in a hospital or being seated at a banquet. I enjoyed watching her gracefulness as it was displayed through the news coverage of her philanthropic efforts. What a lovely lady! She was consistently poised and well presented to the entire world. Princess Di was a tall woman (5'10") who stood tall and proud. I never observed her slouching when she stood or sat. I adore looking at the plethora of beautiful photographs of her. She was the personification of elegance.

Another role model that comes to mind while thinking of outstanding posture is Audrey Hepburn. Miss Hepburn, my favorite actress, was also a tall lady (5'7") but she never slouched. She was a dancer who stood up straight and held her shoulders back. Watch a few of her movies and witness firsthand the loveliness she displayed through her picturesque physical presentation. One of my favorite movies is *Breakfast at Tiffany's*. As you watch the movie, be attentive to the way she stands, sits, and walks.

Who do you think of when you try to think of someone who displays excellent posture? I think of my mentor, Dr. Earline Pinckley. She has the best posture of any woman I know. She stands and sits tall and holds her shoulders back. Whether you are a man or woman, maintain good posture. Do not "let down" when you are tired. Excellent posture makes you appear confident, energetic, and in control.

Sit and Stand Properly

I learned to sit and stand properly through yoga classes taught by my friend Fabian Holland. Yoga teaches participants how to stand or sit for indefinite periods of time, utilizing what is known as the Mountain Pose. This pose is accomplished when one stands with legs slightly parted with one's weight evenly distributed on both legs. The pelvis is slightly rolled under—not swayed backward—and shoulders are held back. When achieving this pose, one is able to stand for extended periods of time. While in the principal's office, you will be supervising events on a daily basis. I strongly recommend you study proper posture techniques through reading or by taking a yoga class. You will learn to sit or stand comfortably.

My piano teacher also taught me how to sit properly. She stressed the importance of sitting up straight in order to master the technique of piano playing. I still strive to model this correct posture when sitting in a chair on a stage at an awards program. Be dignified, as principal, when on the stage representing your school. Ladies should especially remember to sit properly when wearing a dress or skirt. Do not cross your legs. You may, however, cross your ankles while keeping your knees together. Wear slacks or a longer skirt so you will not be fidgeting with your skirt while seated in front of hundreds of people. Ladies and gentlemen should display correct posture while sitting and standing so that your mother, your yoga instructor, and your piano teacher will be proud. You will reap the added benefit of having more energy by standing and sitting correctly.

> *Mountain Pose is the foundation of all standing yoga poses. Stand tall in the present moment as you offer your grateful heart to the world.*

> —Fabian Holland, yoga instructor

CONFIDENCE

Do you have confidence? It is hard to define what one looks like when one possesses confidence. Pause for a moment and think of a person you know who is confident. Consider the following questions:

1. Why do you consider this person to be confident? Is this because of the person's presentation? Is it because of the language this person utilizes daily?
2. In your opinion, would others describe you as confident? Why or why not?

I can think of several people who are confident. One person who immediately comes to my mind who exemplifies a confident man is my husband, Wholey. Wholey is consistently calm and controlled. Regardless of the situation, he is in command and seems to have the answer to any problem presented to him. For example, when we remodeled a small cabin on Smith Lake, we encountered a multitude of challenges. Wholey carefully researched issues and developed a course of action effortlessly and with confidence as he directed the workers.

As principal, you will be called to make numerous decisions each day. Have confidence in your actions and exude authority and leadership while you serve in the principal's office. You do not have to be the expert on every subject, but you should present yourself in a manner that exhibits a sense that you are comfortably in charge of each situation that arises. Confident principals:

- Stay calm
- Maintain control
- Make decisions
- Speak with authority

CLOTHES

> *Wear not your clothes foul, ripped or dusty, but see that they be brushed once every day, at least, and take heed that you approach not to any uncleanness.*

> —George Washington, 1745

Principal Sid Ingram always dressed professionally. If school was in session, he always wore a suit or a coat and tie. During the summer months, he could be seen wearing a Grissom High School football sports shirt with khaki pants. When a visitor entered the office, he or she could immediately tell who the principal was by virtue of his appearance and confidence. His attractive clothes were always freshly ironed. He wore dress shoes that were polished and in good repair. I never saw him wearing dirty, scuffed shoes with worn heels. He dressed this way every day he served in the principal's office. When I saw him away from school, for example, on the weekends, he was casually dressed, but he was well groomed then also. He would be seen wearing pressed khaki pants and a shirt with a nice sweater. Again, his shoes were in good repair, whether tennis shoes or casual shoes.

Clothes Are Important

Whether you are male or female, clothes are important in your role as principal. Dress professionally. Remember that you are a role model; your students, faculty, and parents will be watching what you wear. Women should remember that the office is no place to try to look sexy or youthful with clothing choices. There should be a marked difference in the way a woman dresses at the office and the way she dresses for a date. Do not try to dress like you are twenty when you are fifty years old. I guarantee you that others will ridicule your efforts if you try to achieve this look.

Be modest at work and remember your purpose in being there is not to look sexy or trendy. Your job is to serve as the principal; strive to divert as much attention away from you as possible and focus on whatever may be the task at hand.

Be a Lady, Dear

Because of the realization that, as a woman, I am a role model for my female students in matters of dress, I always strive to be ladylike and wear feminine clothes often. In particular, I probably wear dresses and skirts more frequently than I wear slacks. I once spoke to a gentleman who saw me at meetings on a regular basis, and he remarked how it was refreshing for him to see me because I dressed like a lady. He went on to discuss how dress standards in general have declined in our society and people seem to dress for comfort, not appearance. He noted he often sees women wearing jeans and t-shirts when he and his wife are out shopping. He said he told his wife that there was nothing prettier than seeing a woman wearing a dress and high-heeled shoes and looking like a lady.

When I was recommended to become the principal at Whitesburg Middle School, I was talking to my mother-in-law about what I was going to wear to the board meeting. She told me to "wear a dress and be a lady, dear." I did wear a dress that night and I continue to try to dress in a professional, ladylike manner each day. Dress professionally and realize you are a role model for your students in matters of dress. Also, dress in what makes you feel most professional whenever you can.

Clothing Recommendations for Men and Women

Below are recommendations for taking care of your wardrobe whether you are a man or woman:

- Buy quality clothing items that will stand the test of time and look good at the end of the day. For example, linen dresses are probably not the best choice for women in the principal's office. By the end of the day, you will look like a wrinkled mess if you wear that fabric. Perhaps the linen dress would be a good choice for an awards program.
- My suggested "must haves" for women and men are: navy blazer, khaki pants/skirt, gray pants/skirt, white blouses/shirts, black suit, sleeveless sweater vest that coordinates with your school colors, and tweed suit and/or pants.
- Men should purchase long socks so that if they cross their legs, no leg will be exposed.
- Minimize your wardrobe by selecting colors that complement your skin tone and hair color. There are numerous books and television shows regarding how to select clothes that look good on you. One of my favorite books is John T. Malloy's *Dress for Success.*
- Purchase the basics and avoid trendy styles and colors. You will be able to co-ordinate your clothes more efficiently if you have items that will mix and match.
- Only keep clothes in your closet that fit, are comfortable, and look good. Also, these clothes should be in perfect condition. The minute you notice a button missing on a shirt, either repair it or send it to the dry cleaners to do so. If you have an item that is stained or beyond repair, throw it away.
- Find a reputable dry cleaner to take care of your clothes. Budget money in your monthly expenses to cover this cost. My husband and I allocate $70 monthly for dry cleaning expenses. Men's shirts look ten times better when they are laundered professionally. Pants will last longer if taken to the dry cleaners instead of washing and drying. Remove clothes from the dry cleaning bags when you get home. Natural fibers do not need to be enclosed within the dry cleaning bag.
- Take care of your clothes and remove any item that is not used from your closet. When you transition your clothes from summer to fall, try on your clothes before placing them in the closet. Give any unused items that are in good shape to a worthy charity of your choice. Carefully fold these items and place them in a XXL storage bag. Mark the bag with a permanent pen and label the size of the garments enclosed.
- Organize your closet to minimize the time you spend selecting clothes for the day. Group all pants together. Put blouses/shirts together. Arrange these items by color.
- Fold all sweaters neatly, arranged by color, as you carefully stack them on the shelves in your closet or in your drawers.

- Replace the lighting in your closet to bright lights that simulate sunlight. This tip has enabled me to really see in my closet and distinguish between dark blue and black.
- Consider investing in a closet organizer if you do not presently have your closet's space maximized. You may be able to double your space with this small investment.
- Launder your clothes each week lovingly. Wash whites together and quickly remove them from the dryer and fold in order to eliminate wrinkling. Wash delicate items together and let these items such as undergarments and tops air-dry. Wash colored items together and do not overdry these items.
- Purchase a hook that attaches to your door so that you can select your clothes the night before and hang them for easy access. This will save you time each morning. I dislike standing in the closet in a stupor trying to decide what I will wear each day. When I pre-select my clothes, this is one less detail I must worry about in the morning when time is coveted.
- Make your closet an attractive, clean space. I prefer to have white or neutral painted walls in my closet so that I can see the color of my clothes. Remove scuffs on the walls and doors by using Mr. Clean Magic Eraser. This is one of the best products I have ever used. I cleaned my entire closet with this product when we moved into our present home. Keep your closet dust-free by regular vacuuming or sweeping. Don't forget to dust the baseboards in the closet.
- Invest in a steamer. Use it regularly to erase wrinkles from clothes. Never wear wrinkled clothes.

ACCESSORIES

In addition to serving as the epitome of a well-dressed principal, Mr. Ingram's accessories were picture-perfect as well. By accessories, I am referring to his tie, belt, handkerchief, watch, ring, and wallet. His tie was not dated. Mr. Ingram wore clothes that were timeless yet fashionable. He wore a simple gold watch and a wedding ring. His quality belt was practical and not worn. His long socks were not thin and frayed; they matched his suit and tie.

Regardless of your individual preferences, while at work, the goal should be to minimize accessories. Again, the idea is to present oneself in a simple, professional manner so that the people with whom you interact leave thinking about the essence of your meeting and not remembering your long red fingernails or the rings you wore on every finger.

Some tips for accessories for women follow:

- Less is more, as they say. In terms of jewelry, wear only a few pieces at a time. It is professional to wear conservative earrings and a simple necklace along with a watch, wedding ring, or college ring.
- A scarf can dress up any outfit; a scarf is the equivalent of a man's tie.

- Belts are needed with pants or skirts that have belt loops attached. Match the tones of your jewelry, watch, and belt buckle. If you like to wear silver, you may want to match these items. However, some people prefer an eclectic assortment of jewelry and tones. Whichever you choose, you should be discreetly adorned with accessories.
- Purses should not be distractions. Professional women usually do not carry purses everywhere they go. I remember, years ago, attending a reception for superintendent candidates. One of the ladies walked around for an hour with huge purse on her arm. This was not a good look—trust me. She looked awkward and intimidated. It appeared like she was afraid to lay her purse down because someone might steal it. You can avoid this precarious situation by purchasing jackets, slacks, and skirts with pockets when you can. This will make it easy for you to carry a small amount of cash, lipstick, and your keys.
- I usually tuck my keys securely into my waistband while I am walking through the school. Another effective tool I have used is an elastic wristband to attach my keys. You can find these elastic bands at your local hardware or hobby store. Try to not overload this key holder. Simply carry the keys you need for the day.
- Invest in a quality, professional briefcase or bag. Black is a perfect color. It does not clash with other colors you are wearing and it does not show dirt. You will be glad you invested in a quality bag. There are numerous choices available. I have a microfiber bag that I adore. You can find nice leather bags in a number of department stores. Select one that fits your needs.
- Do not leave large amounts of money in your bag or purse at work. If you leave a wallet in your office, securely lock it in a drawer. More than once, I had to deal with stolen items from employees' offices and purses while at school. Be proactive so that you do not have to deal with this unfortunate occurrence.

WEAR SENSIBLE SHOES

I call my favorite work shoes my Washington Sensible Shoes. They are my black (black patent is my favorite) Ferragamo pumps. They have a two-inch heel and are oh, so comfortable. I can walk all over a school campus and feel good at the end of the day. They are professional shoes, not cute or sexy shoes, and they are practical and sensible. I keep them polished and have the heels replaced at my local shoe repair store when needed.

Professionals, both men and women, in Washington, D.C., and New York can be seen wearing sensible shoes. In fact, Abraham Lincoln was wearing boots on the night he was shot. The boots were black leather with maroon goatskin tops. I too like to wear comfortable black leather boots from time to time. I find them to be practical, smart-looking, and comfortable.

It is important to be comfortable during the day. When I travel, my number-one priority is packing comfortable shoes because I know we will be engaging in a tremendous amount of walking during the trip. I have had the unfortunate experience of being on more than one trip with friends and family where blisters on someone's feet almost ruined the day.

Men Take Better Care of Their Feet Than Women

Generally speaking, men take better care of their feet than women. They consistently wear comfortable shoes that fit. Therefore, it is rare to hear men talk about painful feet or see them on crutches or with a boot due to foot surgery. Women, on the other hand, tend to abuse their feet by insisting on wearing high-heeled, stylish shoes.

Not only is it physically painful to wear high-heeled, contortionist shoes to school, it also can promote a negative image. In order to be a highly visible principal, I recommend wearing comfortable shoes so that you will be able to walk all over the campus as needed. Keep a pair of tennis shoes in your office to wear when you need to go to the playground or football field.

Go for Comfort

There is an infinite array of attractive, comfortable shoes available for men and women. There is simply no reason to suffer with foot pain while serving in the principal's office. Wear sensible shoes and walk; accomplish your tasks during the day without the pain associated with wearing "pretty" shoes that are ruining your feet.

(12)

OUTPUT

Manners and Communication

Drink not, nor talk with your mouth full; neither gaze about you while you are drinking.

—George Washington, 1745

We want to have impeccable manners and positive communication skills in order to welcome others and make them comfortable while in our presence. There is simply no substitute for good manners. Possessing polished manners will assist you in your day-to-day meetings with others and at social events that you will need to attend. Those with impeccable manners help themselves because they display sensitivity toward others, while those without manners prevent themselves from moving forward. People who are socially illiterate and unable to carry a conversation with another person only hinder their efforts to solve problems and promote their goals.

MANNERS

It seems some manners have slipped by the wayside in the last few years. It is fairly common in our busy culture to send a wedding or baby gift and never receive a thank-you note acknowledging that the person received it. Likewise, I have heard my friends lament that some people do not seem to know that RSVP (or *répondez s'il vous plaît*) means that you should please respond, no matter the case, rather than responding only if you are not attending (a request for this type of reply is phrased "Regrets only"). They issue invitations with this request only to be disappointed with the lack of response. Consequently, they plan social events not certain of the number of attendees. RSVP invitations require a response from you. You should reply whether or not you plan to attend the event. The host will have to pay whether you attend or not—and you do not want the host to incur unnecessary expense due to your lack of response.

As the leader of your school, it is imperative that you know the basic expected manners in today's society. You should not have to think about manners; they should be second nature to you. Manners can be acquired by reading and observing others. The more often you practice displaying manners, the more comfortable you will feel using them in public.

You are teaching students manners each day simply by displaying them in their presence. Students are watching you. They watch you at school and everywhere you go. They see how you treat others. They listen to your words and emulate your actions.

Remember to say *please* and *thank you*. Respond to invitations. Remember to write a note of appreciation. Know the basics of dining. Know which fork to use (start with the outside fork) and which way to pass the bread (to the right). Know how to properly shake hands (see below). Know how to wear your name badge (on your right lapel so that when you shake hands with people they can easily see your name). Know how to introduce others (see below). There are a number of etiquette books you can read and study in order to improve or review manners. Emily Post, Amy Vanderbilt, and a host of others have written etiquette books to assist us in our quest to be genteel in today's world. By reviewing these basic manners, you will be prepared and confident in the myriad social situations in which you will find yourself while serving in the principal's office. Remember that you are representing your school in all settings.

Hospitality is making your guests feel at home, even if you wish they were.

—Author unknown

Manners must adorn knowledge and smooth its way in the world; without them it is like a great rough diamond, very well in a closet by way of curiosity, and also for its intrinsic value; but most prized when polished.

—Chesterfield in *Dictionary of Thoughts* (1877)

Know How to Make Introductions

It is courteous to begin conversations and meetings with proper introductions to ensure that the people involved in the exchange know each other. Formal introductions in a professional setting follow a hierarchy. The person in a lower position is introduced to the person in a higher position. Begin the introduction with the name of the person in the higher position. Slowly pronounce names to be sure that each person correctly captures the introduction.

For example, when I had the opportunity to meet President Jimmy Carter, his assistant introduced me by saying, "President Carter, I would like for you to meet Dr. Jan Harris, Superintendent of Cullman City Schools in Alabama." In your school, if you have a dignitary, such as the mayor, visiting your school, you would introduce others to the mayor by saying, "Mayor Green, I would like for you to meet Ms. Jayne Barnett. Ms. Barnett is the principal of Cullman Middle School." If you are conducting a parent-teacher conference, begin by making sure that each person involved in the conference knows each other. Always begin introductions with the parent because the parent is your honored guest. In a business setting, the client would be treated in this manner. For example, "Ms. Smith, I would like for you to meet Ms. Freeman. Ms. Freeman teaches your child, Lance, English."

When you are being introduced to another person, restate the individual's name. It will help you to remember the name. When I was introduced to President Carter, I replied, "President Carter, I am honored to meet you." In a social setting, try to give the people you are introducing a tidbit of information to begin a conversation. For example, if you know they both graduated from the same university, you might share this fact at the time of introduction.

Know How to Shake Hands

In 1995, my father and I traveled to Europe. It was at this time that I learned how to properly shake hands. While we were in Paris, our group toured Notre Dame Cathedral. It is an amazingly beautiful cathedral! During our tour, President Bill Clinton arrived with the French ambassador. We were shocked because we had no idea the president of the United States was even in France, much less in the same cathedral with us!

President Clinton walked like a president, confident and poised. He was our president. He was my president. He was elected to lead our great country. Here was the *president of the United States* walking ten feet away from me while I was in a foreign country! It was a moving experience for my father and me. The Secret Service official walked through the crowd and parted the group like the Red Sea was parted for Moses and the Israelites. Each member of the Secret Service had his back to the president and thus formed a line while he walked between them. Instead of being nervous or in a hurried state, President Clinton strolled through the crowd purposefully, as if he was enjoying each step of his visit while connecting with people in the cathedral at that moment.

As he walked by me, I reached through the crowd with my arm and yelled "Mr. President!" He turned to me, smiled and extended his hand to mine and gave me a genuine, warm handshake. He shook hands with several other people including the teenaged girl standing to my left. Afterward, she and I looked at each other with tears streaming down our cheeks. You see, it had nothing to do with Bill Clinton the person or with the political party to which he belonged. It had everything to do with the fact that we were Americans in a foreign land and our president was there and he touched us. It was a memorable experience.

Know How to Shake Hands

Men should not shake the hand of a woman unless she extends her hand first. If she does so, be gentle as to not squeeze her hand too tightly. Some older women have arthritis in their hands and it is painful when you do so. Also, many women wear rings and it hurts when someone squeezes their hand or fingers.

Reach forward with an open hand. Make sure the web of your hand, the area between the thumb and index finger, meet the web of the other person's hand. Once they meet, gently, but firmly close your fingers around the other person's hand and squeeze it. Hold the squeeze for a couple of seconds. You don't want to hold the handshake too long, but you do want the individual to feel that you are sincere with your handshake. Your handshake should reveal that you are glad to see this person!

I teach my students and aspiring administrators how to shake hands properly. It surprises me to realize how many people do not know how to shake hands properly. As principal, you will be shaking hands with parents and visitors at your school every day. If you are a high school principal, you will be shaking hands with each senior as he/she walks across the stage at graduation. You want the recipient of your special handshake to feel important. Practice your handshake until you feel comfortable with it.

COMMUNICATION

We are what we repeatedly do. Excellence, then, is not an act, but a habit.

—Aristotle

The Importance of a Smile

Before you say one word, people can see your attitude and disposition through the window you wear on your face. This window is your facial expression. Smiling conveys a positive demeanor while frowning conveys a negative demeanor. Read the questions below and choose the answer that best describes your disposition:

1. Would your colleagues and friends describe you as friendly or standoffish?
   a. People think I am friendly and tell me so frequently.
   b. I am a serious person and do not have time to be overly friendly.

2. Do you usually smile or frown or wear a neutral facial expression?
   a. I smile most of the time.
   b. I have a neutral expression on my face.
   c. I am not a happy person and therefore I frown frequently.
3. How would a colleague describe you to another person?
   a. She/he is the friendly person who immediately puts you at ease with her smiles and laughter.
   b. She/he is the sad-looking, quiet person.

If you selected A for the answer to each question, you smile often, which is good for social interactions. However, if you selected B or C for your answers, then I would like to encourage you to consider smiling more often. I am not suggesting that you become overly friendly or happy; I am simply asking you to consider how others view you in the world. If you do not smile often, why is that? Could you work on smiling more frequently?

Smile. You don't always have to be the serious or intimidating principal. Smiles help us to relax. Smiles help others to relax as well. As they say, "You will catch more flies with honey." Smiling may help teachers, parents, and students feel more comfortable around you, thus they may be more likely to bring you their small issues before they are become enormous or out-of-control issues. Genuinely demonstrate kindness and empathy to others by smiling when you speak to them or acknowledge their presence.

Body Language

A smile is one way to convey a positive or negative message with your body language. There are other ways in which you can communicate with your body language. For example, have you ever corrected a student or your own child and had him or her roll his or her eyes while you were speaking? Have you ever had a person cross his or her arms during a confrontation as if to indicate this person is shutting your thoughts and opinions out of their consideration? Have you ever tried to talk to someone who will not look at you while you are speaking? These are all examples of negative body language.

On the other hand, have you ever tried to talk to someone and had that person give you his 100 percent attention? Did the good listener nod while you talked as if she agreed with your sentiments? Have you ever had a good listener lean forward while you were talking as if to say, "tell me more"? These are all examples of positive body language.

While you are in the principal's office, you will spend the majority of your time communicating with others. Communication will be verbal, nonverbal, and written. A person who possesses exemplary communication skills will be better equipped for success in the principal's office because such a large part of the principal's life is spent communicating with others. A polished principal will glide through difficult situations if he/she is skillful in this key area.

Verbal Communication

Have you heard the admonition to listen more than you speak? I like the reminder that God gave us two ears and one mouth, therefore, we should listen twice as much as we speak. Throughout each day, people will bring you information verbally. They expect you to be a good listener. If you are not a good listener, take heart: Listening skills can be learned and improved.

A few tips for effective verbal communication follow:

1. Listen, listen, listen to the other person and do not interrupt.
2. Give the person with whom you are meeting your full attention. Close your office door and silence your cell phone or Blackberry. Listen to the person completely as he or she conveys the issue at hand. Again, do not interrupt while the other person is speaking.
3. Take notes as you listen.
4. Display positive body language. Lean forward; give eye contact. Nod when you can agree with a comment being made during the conference.
5. After the person finishes talking (this can be 15–30 minutes), restate the issue as you understand it and ask for validation of your understanding of the issue.
6. At the conclusion of the meeting, ask the person why he/she is sharing this information with you. Does the person simply want you to be aware of this information, or does the person want you to go to the teacher and investigate this matter?
7. Be careful with your response. Speak as if all parties involved are actually in the room as you are speaking. Pretend you are being recorded as you give your opinion of the matter. Give responses that you would be proud to have replayed in front of the teacher, superintendent, or student. Would you be proud of your response if it were printed in its entirety in your local newspaper?
8. Do not feel pressed to render an immediate opinion on the matter. Often, I will tell the person I will look into this matter and get back with him/her within a week. Keep your promise. If you told the parent you would investigate and get back with him/her in a week, be sure to do so. Write a reminder in your calendar.
9. Never address anonymous complaints. I learned a valuable lesson by addressing a complaint by a teacher who wished to remain anonymous. Teacher #1 reported an ethics violation against teacher #2 to me. Teacher #2 denied the allegation. Teacher #1 did not want to get involved. My relationship with teacher #2 was damaged as a consequence of teacher #1's lack of courage and my naivety in addressing an anonymous complaint. Never get in the middle of petty politics by addressing anonymous complaints. If the complainer is unwilling to give his/her name, then be unwilling to address the issue. In the judicial system, the accused does have a right to know who his/her accuser is in his day of court.

10. If you have a person in your office who is a regular complainer, consider having another person, such as the assistant principal, sit in the conference. This often keeps the complainer more on target and more guarded with what they say.

Speak not evil of the absent, for it is unjust.

—George Washington, 1745

13

TIME AND MEMORY

Time stays long enough for anyone who will use it.

—Leonardo da Vinci

One of my former students, Colby Carter, was an exceptional student who graduated as one of the top academic students of his class at Grissom High School, a school nationally recognized for its academic excellence. Additionally, he was a state-champion tennis player and a leader in student organizations at school. After graduation practice, he invited the counselor and me for a root beer float at a local restaurant. While enjoying the delightful visit and the float, I commended Colby for his outstanding accomplishments and asked him to what did he attribute his success.

Colby explained that he tried to use his time wisely each day and that every day he did one thing for himself. He said, "Today my 'one thing' is having a root beer float with you and Mrs. Prefling." I have often thought about Colby's wisdom in this simple discipline he mastered so early in life. Work hard but do one thing each day for yourself. In the midst of "busyness," I will often ask myself, "What have I done for me today?"

CONTROL YOUR USE OF TIME

While you are serving in the principal's office, people will regularly request "just a few minutes" of your time. You must learn to control your use of time or you will never complete tasks on your list of important things to do each day. Some tips to manage your time follow.

Allow no more than thirty minutes for each conference. If Lee Iacocca could manage Chrysler using this principle, then you can manage your school while practicing it. Have your secretary knock on the door or call you on your intercom to help you stay on schedule and signify the end of the conference, if needed. After summarizing the points of the conference, stand up and thank the person for coming. The other person will understand that when you stand, you are indicating the meeting is coming to a close. Take as much time as needed to be kind and attentive, but strive to control meetings so that emotional individuals do not restate issues again and again and waste time.

Create rules for your time management. For example, I established a rule to not meet with a parent until the parent had already met with the teacher. This significantly reduced the time I spent in conferences. Parents needed to talk to the teacher; by talking to the teacher, usually this resolved the conflict and there was no reason for the parent to meet with me, the principal.

Determine your most productive time of the day and block this time (1–2 hours) for reading and paperwork. Schedule time in your day to observe classes and also time to return calls and meet with others as needed. If you do not schedule some time each day to do your necessary tasks, you will find that each and every day will go by without you accomplishing any of your required tasks. It can easily happen because you will be pulled at daily by teachers, parents, and students.

Stay on task until the task is completed—just like a bank teller. If you are in the middle of sending an email when someone interrupts you at your door, finish the email before giving your attention to this person.

Strive to complete tasks as early as possible. Do not procrastinate. Procrastination drains you intellectually since you are continually thinking about the task that is yet to be done.

While we are talking about time, remember to be on time for meetings and events. Start leaving your office thirty minutes before you actually need to leave and you should be able to arrive at your meeting on time, with a relaxed, calm demeanor.

Dost thou love life? Then do not squander time, for that is the stuff life is made of.

—Benjamin Franklin, a maxim prefixed to
Poor Richard's Almanac in 1757

MEMORY

Do you struggle trying to remember names of students and others? How do you remember names? I try to remember the names of others through association. I use a mapping technique to help me connect new information with information I already possess. For example, I met Suzanne when I moved to Cullman. I also met her parents, Wayne and Elaine. Suzanne works for Vicki and is married to Terry who works at the bank. Their three children attend school at the middle and high school and Auburn University. By mapping information related to Suzanne, I am better able to remember the other individuals. East Elementary Principal David Wiggins also utilizes mapping techniques to remember names. I have seen this at work when I visit the school and he displays the most impressive recollection of students' names.

It helps me to remember names by repeating the person's name after the initial introduction. Also, I am not shy about asking someone's name. People know that you interact with hundreds of people on a daily basis. It is no shame to simply ask an individual, "I'm sorry, but I cannot recall your name." I am constantly trying to improve in the area of name recollection, but these little techniques help me tremendously.

Keep a Little Black Book

Instead of trying to hold important facts in my mind, I enlist the help of a journal I call my Little Black Book. My dear mother-in-law, Patricia Harris, gave me one of the best tips for organizing information I have ever received. She showed me a small journal that she kept to document important dates, such as when she purchased a household item. Her journal also included bank and insurance information. Pat said that this journal helped her to remember when she purchased items and enabled her to keep up with her business. In addition to household information, she recorded medical information and other dates of importance in this journal.

I immediately embraced this idea and have used a household journal like Pat did ever since she taught me how to do so. I also adapted this idea for the principal's office. I suggest you also use a journal to help you house the important information about your school. At work, my Little Black Book contains information such as who I hired each year along with who retired. It also includes donation information: who donated money or gifts, along with the date and a description of the gift. Also, I document when I mailed a thank-you card to the giver. An example of an entry in my Little Black Book is located in appendix C.

Use Your Little Black Book to Assist with Discipline Matters

I found this Little Black Book to be effective in the discipline arena when I served as a middle school principal. One day, the counselor brought three young men to my office and told me that they were guilty of making fun of a female student because of her weight. This was a serious matter and I do not condone bullying in any form. I believe all educators are the equalizers in the schoolhouse and it is our responsibility to protect all of our children.

I wanted to convey to these boys that this behavior was unacceptable and would not be tolerated. I dramatically walked behind my desk and picked up my Little Black Book, and explained to them how wrong it was for them to act this way. I told them that if it happened again, I would have to write their names in my book and it would be documented forever that they acted in this way. Their eyes were big and wide as they listened to me intently. This was the last time they mistreated the female student.

I also used the Little Black Book to document the names of students who were on probation or expelled. I did not include every little detail; I only included the big matters that I wanted to be able to reference if needed. You can also do the same with personnel matters and awards and honors your school receives. Keep a Little Black Book. It will become an invaluable tool for your use.

January 13, 1996—purchased washer and dryer from Sears for $800, purchased service warranty. Service contract number: 123ABC.

—Sample journal entry from Patricia Harris

SUMMARY OF PART II
KEYS FOR PHYSICAL BALANCE

1. Take care of your body. Just as you must maintain your vehicle, it is imperative that you take care of your body though rest, play, and exercise, as well as through preventive measures such as having physicals.
2. Fuel your body with nutritious food each day. Avoid junk food.
3. Deliver the best physical presentation you can as principal of your school. Arrive at school each day refreshed, well groomed, and attractively dressed in professional attire.
4. Display impeccable manners that will put others at ease.
5. Utilize effective communication techniques. Listen more than you talk when meeting with others.
6. Effectively use your time each day in order to maximize your task accomplishments during a day. Do not waste time by standing around talking unnecessarily. Give others the time they need when they are asking for help, but manage this time efficiently by listening, taking notes, and summarizing the details of the conference.
7. Do not rely upon your own memory. Enlist the help of a Little Black Book and use mapping techniques to help you remember others names and important information.

III

INTELLECTUAL BALANCE

Within the perimeter of the intellectual domain, we find tasks such as education, work, study, organizing, analyzing, and writing. The need for continual growth in this area is paramount. Growth comes by simply reading books, magazines, journals, and newspapers to keep up with changes in education and current events. It can be obtained by taking courses to further your education. Also, growth occurs by learning from others. Because you will be dealing with a diverse group of people with varied backgrounds and interests, it is important that you have a global perspective by being culturally literate and generally informed in areas other than education. Time must be allocated for continual growth in the intellectual domain because it is easy to stay consumed with the day-to-day problems at your school and thus not make the effort to improve in this area.

> *They who have read about everything are thought to understand everything, too, but it is not always so; reading furnishes the mind only with materials of knowledge; it is thinking that makes what we read ours. We are of the ruminating kind, and it is not enough to cram ourselves with a great load of collections —we must chew them over again.*
>
> —Channing in *Dictionary of Thoughts* (1877)

14

BE PROFESSIONAL
AND STICK TO THE BOOK

You are the principal of your school. Serving as principal is a serious responsibility. Do the job that is set before you with professionalism and expertise. Understand the expectations of the job and the legal foundation for the decisions you will make as you guide your school into the future.

UNDERSTAND YOUR ROLE AND RESPONSIBILITIES

Before you walk through the door of the principal's office, make certain that you have a thorough understanding of the role and responsibilities you are about to assume. Usually, the board of education will have a job description on file for your perusal. It will clearly state the minimum expectations for your job performance, and it will clarify your responsibilities as principal. It will probably also state the qualifications needed for the position and to whom you will report. Some of the minimum expectations for the principal may include:

1. Overseeing the instructional program of your school and scheduling classes.
2. Maintaining the facility and campus.
3. Maintaining effective discipline and a safe and orderly atmosphere conducive to learning.
4. Interviewing and recommending employees for hiring.
5. Evaluating employees.
6. Managing school finances.
7. Providing professional development for staff.
8. Possessing effective communication and interpersonal skills.

9. Communicating high expectations for student and staff performance.
10. Maintaining an effective extracurricular program (for secondary students).

Understand the Limitations of Your Authority

Know the scope of your role in the organization and the limits of your authority. Understand which responsibilities fall under your jurisdiction and which responsibilities fall under the authority at a higher level. Focus on the areas for which you are responsible. If you are unsure of whether you have the authority to make a certain decision at your school, explain the situation to your supervisor in order to avoid overstepping your boundaries. This will not be a frequent occurrence but you will encounter situations that will not be covered in a book or board policy. Do not be timid in seeking clarification when you need it as you begin your tenure as principal. As you progress through the years, you will become more confident about the areas for which you are responsible.

And, while we are talking about your role and responsibilities, make sure that those you supervise understand *their* roles and responsibilities. Periodically review this information with employees to ensure that they also have a clear understanding of your expectations. By being proactive and communicating clearly, your school will function better. We all work more efficiently if we have clearly defined roles and responsibilities.

Understand Your District's Organizational Chart

A wise principal will carefully study and understand the organizational structure of the school district prior to assuming the new duties. I have watched the demise of several colleagues who failed to understand their role and responsibilities and the district's organizational chart. First, understand the chain of command. In a small school district, you may be directly supervised by the superintendent. In a large school district, you may report to the director of elementary or secondary education. If you report to the director, you should always communicate with this person unless there is some unusual circumstance. Principals, ultimately, report to the superintendent. The superintendent reports to the board of education. Note that principals do not report directly to board members. This is an area that can be problematic. Your school district will most likely have an organizational chart that you can study. It may be similar to the chart shown in figure 14.1.

From time to time, you will communicate with a board member who may call or visit your school or you may see the board member while out in the community. During the exchange, he or she may ask you questions or bring up areas of concern. After the visit, communicate the content of the visit to your superintendent or supervisor so that he or she will have knowledge of the visit. Do not try to be friends or socialize with board members. I have never witnessed a successful situation where a principal courted board members in an effort to get ahead. Circumventing the organizational chart can be hazardous to your job

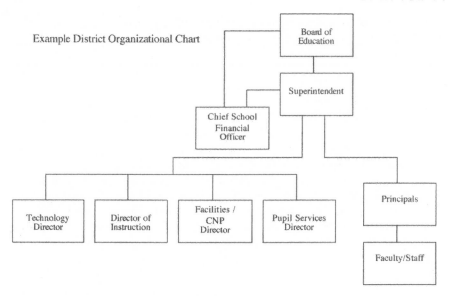

Example District Organizational Chart

Figure 14.1. "Example District Organizational Chart"

longevity! Be professional and let the superintendent work with the board of education while you focus on your areas of responsibility.

Be Loyal to Your Superintendent and the School System for which You Work

Be loyal to the system for which you work, and thus pays your salary, and adhere to the system's ideals. Strive to be a good representative of your system at all times. Do not forget that this system gave you this opportunity to serve in the principal's office. You will have multiple opportunities to hear others criticize the leadership above you. Do not participate in this negative banter, as it will not be productive. If you strongly disagree with a decision or policy, talk to your supervisor in a private setting about the issue. You may not change the policy, but at least you will have been true to yourself in addressing the issue respectfully and professionally.

> *Before you walk through the door of the principal's office, understand the role and responsibilities you are about to assume.*
>
> —Jan Irons Harris

STICK TO THE BOOK

The U.S. Constitution does not mention education; therefore, education is a state function that is controlled at the state level through the legislative process. The state department of education oversees the educational process within your state. Federal programs are simply controlled through financial appropriations. For example, if your school is eligible for federal funds, it will be bound to adhere to federal guidelines in order to access these funds. The written guides that provide an operational foundation for conducting business include:

1. State and federal laws. (Many of these laws will be reflected in your system's board policy manual.)
2. State administrative code.
3. System board policy.

Stay abreast of changes in the law and in policy. When laws change, your superintendent should make appropriate recommendations to the board of education to update the policy manual for your system. Your system's policy manual should be on your desk because you will use it as a reference on a daily basis. The policy manual is a bible for all school principals. Review it periodically to guide you in your decision-making. Relying upon board policy makes your job much easier. For example, discipline decisions will be not be based on your personal opinion. Your decisions will be consistently based on board policy.

Create a Student Handbook

If your school does not have a student handbook, create one with input from your student council (you probably would not have a student council in a primary school, though), teachers, and parents. This handbook should be in concert with your board policy, of course. Proof this handbook and ask one of your English teachers to edit it. After it is printed, distribute it to all students and have them sign a form acknowledging receipt of this important document.

Review the contents of the handbook with all students each year, either in small groups or in a general assembly. General expectations for behavior should be delineated. The student handbook will also address issues specific to your school, such as checkout procedures. If a student violates a rule listed in the handbook, there will be no misunderstanding. The student will know the behavior is not allowed because you communicated your expectations for behavior through the student handbook at the start of the year. It is helpful to also list penalties for various discipline problems per your school system's board policy.

When I served as assistant principal and principal, I found this handbook to be an invaluable tool for daily use. Keep it on your desk along with your board policy to easily access and reference during parent and student conferences. More than once, during my tenure as principal, a parent literally begged me to not punish his/her child. I kindly explained that I was bound by my contract to uphold board policy. For example, if a student was in my office due to smoking on campus, I showed the parents the board policy that says that smoking is not allowed. Then, I showed the consequences also listed in the board policy. Since I am employed by the board that made this policy, I must enforce this policy. Parents generally understand this principle.

Do not stray from these important documents; they provide the foundation on which you will govern your school. Avoid the tendency to "preach" to others about your personal beliefs when disciplining students or reprimanding employees. Stick to the book. See chapter 18 for more information related to student discipline.

Be as you wish to seem.

—Socrates

(15)

HAVE A PLAN

Every single day in the principal's office is a busy day. In order to maximize your time and energy, utilize your organizational skills in order to manage the business of school administration. One of the tasks you will need to manage is the completion of numerous plans and reports. Be familiar with annual plans and reports that are due to your central office and state department of education. Some of these reports will be related to federal programs, student services (such as attendance and graduation information), curriculum, assessment, finance, technology, career tech, special education, safety, discipline, transportation, athletics, child nutrition, professional development, personnel, and accreditation.

A PLAN FOR YOUR PLANS

Make a chronological list of these required plans and reports in your Little Black Book (see chapter 13 and appendix C for more info on your Little Black Book). Post these due dates electronically in your Outlook calendar as a recurring event so that you can schedule these each year. Outlook will then send you a reminder the month before the report will be due to your state department of education, and you will not forget about them during busy times.

Review existing emergency plans, in detail, when you become the principal and periodically review them thereafter to see if they can be improved. In addition to having a plan on paper with the input of your faculty and staff, think about how you, as principal, would manage such a situation.

Dedicate time to think about the possible plans that could be needed and devise a plan to help you prepare for such an unimaginable event. For example, create an emergency plan that details how you would handle an intruder in the building. Create a plan that delineates how you will handle a severe weather incident such as a tornado or earthquake. Even if this plan will be covered in your safety plan, make sure your role is properly covered and you know, in your own mind, what steps you would take in this critical situation. Also, think about your role, as principal, during a bomb threat or a fire. Personalize your school plans by asking yourself questions such as:

- How will I communicate to my faculty, staff, and students in the event of a power outage?
- Do I need to purchase a bullhorn for emergency use?
- Where do I keep the emergency plans?
- Do I have floor plans? Where are they?
- Where is the safest location in my school in case of a tornado? Do I have maps posted to clearly communicate these safe areas to faculty, staff, and students?
- Do I have regularly scheduled drills to help prepare in case of fire or tornado or in case we truly need to have a lockdown?
- Do I have emergency contact numbers for the superintendent, the police, fire department, and news stations? Do I have the phone numbers of faculty and staff?
- How do I communicate with my staff? Do I have radio connectivity or cell phones? Do teachers have a phone in each room? Do we have a phone tree in place?
- Are exterior doors locked, including main and secondary entrances?
- Do I have surveillance cameras in the building? Who monitors these cameras? Can the police also view these cameras from their office?
- Are rules and expectations for the various possible emergencies clearly communicated periodically by teachers and staff to students?
- Do support staff members such as the lunchroom staff know that they need to also participate in all drills in order to be prepared for a "real" emergency?

PLAN FOR ENFORCING POLICIES AND RULES

Also, think about how you will handle certain situations such as when students misbehave, specifically enforcement of your discipline plan. The implementation of policies and rules for new situations may not be as straightforward as you might think. This can be especially true in discipline cases when the system board policy gives you some latitude in your discipline choices. Again, the key is to strive to be consistent from student to student.

You cannot be prepared for every type of problem, but thinking about potential problems now will serve you well at a later date. For example, say your teacher who sponsors a class or club tells students they may not purchase tickets to the dance at the door, and you support this rule because it allows the sponsor to plan for the number of students attending and it also promotes safety because other students from other schools will not be able to "drop in" to your school dance. Then how are you going to handle this situation if a student arrives and asks for admittance to the dance at the door? Or, say you tell students there will be no early checkouts on the day before a holiday unless they have a doctor's note: How will you handle it when one student shows up without a note but asking to check out?

In other words, when you make a rule—or a plan—think about how it will be enforced. This enforcement will fall to you as the principal. Parents will often visit you when they feel their child has not been treated fairly so you need to be able to articulate the logical and reasonable reasons for your actions that are in accordance with the written school policies. The key is to be able to point out that the rule or plan was clearly delineated to all students and parents.

Additionally, think about how you will handle corrective actions for employees. You will observe areas that will need to be addressed. And I found that, from time to time, employees would report indiscretions of other employees. How will you address this issue if an employee reports to you that a teacher is leaving the building without permission or coming in late to school?

Be prepared as much as possible for trying situations. A fire drill helps to save lives because people do not panic when they have a plan. Creating plans for every imaginable situation in advance will aid you in being better prepared for your challenges each day, even though there will be numerous situations that will demand your immediate attention and judgment.

> *In preparing for battle I have always found that plans are useless, but planning is indispensable.*
>
> —Dwight David Eisenhower

16

BUILD YOUR WINNING TEAM

Alone we can do so little; together we can do so much.

—Helen Keller

As principal, you will build your school's winning team just as a college football coach works to build a winning football team. Coaches scout players and observe them playing during competitions. They talk to other coaches about the player's attitude and work ethic. They examine grades and discipline records. In short, they look at every descriptor possible in order to assist them in determining if this player would be an asset to their team.

Building your winning team at your school is no different. You will build your team one person at a time as you recommend individuals for employment to your superintendent. Each hiring decision you make is critical to your school's overall success. Take this responsibility seriously and invest a good deal of time and effort into the hiring process. This invested time will never be wasted because you do not want to make hiring mistakes. A wise principal's energy is utilized on the front end of personnel management in personnel selection, while unwise principals put endless hours into terminating or working with ineffective employees.

BEFORE THE INTERVIEW

Attend job fairs at local and state universities to reveal potential teacher candidates. Develop relationships with college professors to work together to find personnel. This is especially helpful when you need to replace a vacancy in a subject area that is difficult to fill, such as Latin.

Thoroughly review candidates' work history and minimize hiring mistakes by utilizing a proactive approach to hiring personnel. Additionally, some states, such as Alabama, require that a background check be conducted on all new hires.

The Application

The hiring process begins with a review of potential candidates' resumes and total application packets. Examine the packets carefully and ask yourself the following questions while reviewing each application packet:

- Is it complete?
- Did the candidate use correct grammar?
- Is the packet attractive and neat?
- Are you impressed with the overall presentation of the packet?
- Did the candidate make good grades in college? What was his/her grade point average?
- Did the candidate demonstrate leadership skills in college or high school?
- Does the candidate possess unique skills? For example, did he/she serve as a cheerleader or president of the student council? If so, this individual could be a strong sponsor for these organizations at your school.
- Did the candidate go to college on an athletic scholarship? If so, this candidate may be an excellent coaching candidate.
- Does the candidate speak another language? If so, this could be a help to your school's English-language learners.

Determine Who Will Be Interviewed

After examining the application packets of all who applied for your posted position, determine which applicants will be interviewed. Follow the guidelines for your district and adhere to them closely. For example, your district may require that you interview a certain number of candidates. Strive to have a diverse group from which to interview.

After selecting the candidates you wish to interview, it is time to schedule the event. I like to allow forty-five minutes for each interview I conduct. I prefer to have my administrative assistant schedule the interviews. This step allows me to have another person's view of the candidate prior to the interview. Although I have never mentioned this fact to my assistant, I have recognized the value of this extra input for years. For example, my assistant once told me that a candidate was rude and impatient during her telephone conversation. Another time, my assistant told me of the difficulty she had in conveying directions to the school to the candidate. On another occasion, my assistant commented on the outrageous message on a candidate's answering machine. All of these comments were red flags to me.

THE INTERVIEW

Begin the Interview

When it is time to begin the interview, go to the waiting area of your office and introduce yourself to the candidate. Smile and thank the person for coming to the meeting. Make eye contact. Offer this individual a glass of water or a cup of coffee to make everyone more relaxed. Direct the person to your office. I prefer to interview a candidate in an informal manner by seating myself and the candidate in the set of chairs across from my desk in my office. This is a friendlier approach than having the principal sitting behind the desk or even sitting across from each other at a table. If you do not have a sofa and chairs in your office, sit at a conference table. Put the candidate at the head of the table and sit to the candidate's right. I find this L-format to be friendlier than sitting across from each other with the table serving as a barrier.

Now, notice the person's dress; is it professional? A short skirt or low neckline, as well as extremely flashy clothing or hairstyle, can be a warning sign. Remember that this person is offering his or her best for you to examine during the interview. Most likely, it is not going to get better than this. Is the person well-groomed? Does the person seem at ease? Does he/she exude confidence?

As you begin the interview process, give an overview of the position for which you are interviewing. Have a copy of the job description for the teacher position before you to reference. Speak slowly and distinctly so that the person can capture each and every word you speak. Also, speaking slowly allows the candidate to have time to process and think about the desired answer to the question. Likewise, listen to each word that comes from the candidate. Does the candidate have a good command of the English language? Do the answers make sense? Are the answers appropriate and based on research, educational theory, and best practices?

Potential Interview Questions

A few interview questions I have used during interviews through the years include:

1. Give me a brief overview of your background, experience, and interests.
2. Who is your favorite president and why?
3. Who was your favorite teacher and why?
4. What is your favorite book and why?
5. Describe a perfect lesson in your classroom. Consider asking the candidate to teach you a brief lesson using the office space to do so.
6. What skills do you believe students need to master in the twenty-first century?
7. Did you bring a portfolio with you? If so, examine the entries and ask questions related to the contents presented.
8. Describe your classroom management style.
9. Do you consider yourself a good communicator? How would you communicate with students, parents, administrators? Rate your skills on a scale of 1 to 10, with 10 being the highest score.

10. Are you technologically literate? Rate your skills on a scale of 1 to 10, with 10 being the highest. Do you know how to use email? PowerPoint? Excel? What are a few of your favorite websites/software?
11. Would you describe yourself as a peacemaker or a troublemaker? Why?
12. What additional skills would you bring to our school?
13. Why do you want to work at our school?
14. Do you consider yourself a lifelong learner? What is the last book you read or issue you researched and studied?
15. What hobbies do you enjoy in your spare time?
16. Do you have questions for me?
17. Is there anything you want me to know about you that I have not covered today in my questions?

Questions You May Not Ask

Do not ask the candidate questions on the topics of church affiliation, sexual orientation and marital status, number of children, or political affiliation. Do not discriminate against an individual because of these preferences. You cannot discriminate based on a person's gender, age, religion, color, or race. Never talk about candidates to others unless you are seeking a reference. Be confidential and professional throughout the interview process.

Interview Committees

Some principals like to have a committee of teachers to help interview prospective teachers. If you wish to enlist the committee approach to hiring, narrow the list of potential teacher candidates to three or four individuals before consulting the committee. I do not recommend taking teachers' time from step one to completion of this process. That is your job, as principal. Do as much of the legwork as possible to simplify and streamline the process.

You may want to ask the department head to assist you or have the faculty elect a representative for such a committee. Stay away from personally selecting individuals for these types of tasks. Allowing the faculty to select its representative will earn you respect. Remind the committee that you will make the final decision but you desire their input. Be sure to thank employees on the committee for their time and expertise by providing lunch and also by sending each person a sincere thank-you note.

AFTER THE INTERVIEW

Check References

Check references. It is important. Some people prefer to check references before the interview. I prefer to wait until after interviews to start calling references to obtain recommendations. Network confidentially. For example, if you have a trusted friend from the same hometown as the candidate, ask the friend for a reference on this prospective employee. Was he/she successful in his/her previous job? Why did this candidate leave the previous position? Listen carefully to what the supervisor says and also to what the supervisor does *not* say. Silence may indicate a red warning flag to you.

After carefully verifying the resume and application packet (receiving transcripts, etc.), interviewing and checking references, you will start to form an opinion of this candidate and whether you feel this person would fit the position at your school. Do not get in a hurry when making this decision and do not share your decision with anyone except the superintendent. Do not hesitate to call this individual back for another interview if you need more information. Be able to justify why you selected an individual for a position.

Making Hiring Recommendations

Do not prematurely offer the job to the candidate until the day or so before the board meeting. Communicate to the candidate that this offer is confidential and cannot be shared publicly until the board of education approves the superintendent's recommendation. Do not tell anyone at your school—even your assistant. Be confidential. As they say, loose lips can sink ships. This is a good metaphor to remember. I know of individuals who were not approved for hiring by the board of education because the candidates told people in the community they were getting the such-and-such job. Be careful.

> *Think before you speak; pronounce not imperfectly nor bring out your words too hastily, but orderly and distinctly.*
>
> —George Washington, 1745

WORKING WITH YOUR TEAM MEMBERS

Nurture New Teachers by Mentoring, Meeting, and Observing

Once the board of education hires your new teacher or employee, begin the process of welcoming this individual into your school family. Immediately assign a mentor to this new employee and give an orientation to the school. Don't forget to introduce the culture of your school to the new teacher. Explain how you do things at your school. At Grissom High School, we had a new teacher handbook that detailed a "how to" for just about every situation. If your school does not have a handbook for new teachers, consider creating one for future use.

Each district will have its own process for induction. Of course, the payroll department will educate this person regarding payroll and benefits issues, such as insurance choices. Some districts will provide an orientation for all new teachers. If there is such a program, work within the parameters of this program and build upon this foundation. Be familiar with the content of the orientation so that you can adequately prepare the new teacher for his/her responsibilities.

Hold regular meetings with new teachers and provide topics of interest at each session. Encourage these new individuals all along the way, and let them know that you are checking on them to make sure they have what they need in order to be successful. Stay in touch by visiting the teacher's classroom and familiarizing yourself with the routines and practices taking place. Observe this new teacher formally and informally. Tell the teacher you are available if he/she has questions for you.

Correct, Improve, Discipline

Just as a parent disciplines a child, it is your responsibility to guide this new employee—as well as all employees—at your school. Make this person accountable. If you see a behavior that is undesirable, address it immediately. For example, if a teacher leaves his/her room unattended, talk to the teacher with kindness and explain the procedure for your school when the teacher has an emergency and must leave the room, say, to go to the restroom. Correct in order to improve performance. Remember to reference board policy during your conversations with employees. For example, do not simply tell a new teacher that you expect him or her to be on time. Show the individual the board policy that states teachers are to be in their rooms fifteen minutes before the bell rings each day.

Talk to the individual in his or her classroom privately or in your office. Make sure the door is closed so that others cannot hear your conversation. You would correct a child who ran into the street, and you should correct new teachers by explaining why we do things "this way" at our school.

If the undesirable action continues after you have informally talked to the teacher about it, then hold a formal conference in your office to discuss the issue. Have another administrator, if possible, in the conference to serve as a witness. If the undesirable behavior still continues, put a directive in writing to the teacher. If you have to issue a written directive in order to obtain compliance, this is a warning to you and you will probably need to consider not renewing the nontenured teacher's contract the next year. Communicate personnel problems to your supervisor.

BUILD MORALE AMONG YOUR TEAM

He who guards his lips guards his life . . .

—King Solomon in Proverbs 13:3 (NIV)

Build morale in your school by respecting the individuals who are part of your total team. Never talk to teachers about other teachers. Certified and noncertified employees will come to you from time to time and talk to you about situations that may involve others at your school. Listen, but do not reply or say any derogatory statement about the other person. In fact, try to say something positive about the other person if possible. Think about how you would solve a dispute between two of your children whom you love. One may be totally wrong or both may be partially wrong. Either way, you must sort it all out and help to resolve the conflict with respect and dignity.

Whenever possible, support your staff when parents complain about teachers. Listen to the parents' statements, but again do not make derogatory comments about your faculty and staff to others. Support your staff. Listen during conferences. If you discover your employee made a mistake, tell the person after the conference. I found myself in this situation more than once. I listened to the parent and student. After the teacher and I were alone, I told the teacher to never put me in this position again, because if she did, I would have to correct her in the presence of others. She knew she had made a mistake and apologized profusely. She thanked me for not humiliating her in front of the parent and student. Always encourage your staff and students when they make mistakes and let them know that they can recover from their error through improvement.

Often, a parent will ask, "What are you going to do about Teacher X, and the situation we discussed?" I respond that I will take care of it and it will not happen again (if the teacher is in the wrong). I explain to the parent that I am not going to discuss an employee's personnel history with him/her. They generally understand this position. It would be inappropriate to divulge information in this manner.

Provide Times of Fellowship and Support

In addition to building morale through respect, build morale by having times of fellowship for your faculty and staff. Ask your PTA to help provide breakfast for the staff from time to time. Teachers appreciate this show of appreciation for the hard work they do each and every day. Your PTA can provide encouragement to your staff by providing a card and/or a small treat such as a piece of candy on each staff member's birthday, for example. Build morale by promoting school t-shirts, as well as nicer shirts with the school's logo imprinted upon them. As a faculty, consider participating in one community event together each year. By encouraging fellowship and school spirit attire, you are building the culture of your school. By supporting your faculty and staff and delivering respect to each person, you are building morale and relationships.

When staff members are experiencing difficult personal times, such as a family illness or death, contact the individual and express your concern. Cards, phone calls, and visits are appreciated and remembered. I recently saw a teacher whom I worked with several years ago. After exchanging greetings, she somberly looked at me and said, "You came to my father's visitation. It was out of town, and you and your husband came to his funeral." I did not realize the importance of our actions—nor her deep appreciation—until that moment. Be there for your winning team when they are discouraged or suffering.

Other Key Team Members

Build your winning team by garnering support for your school through effective relationships with parents and community leaders. If you do not currently have a PTA, I strongly encourage you to start a PTA at your school. Enlist the help of your parents in all facets of the school; your students will be the beneficiaries of this extra support. Parents can raise money for special programs or needs at the school. They can provide extra supervision at extracurricular events such as dances.

While I served as principal, I made it a priority to develop a strong relationship with my PTA president. I communicated important issues and events to this leader and made time to keep her (all three of my school's PTA presidents were women) informed. In addition to board meetings, I scheduled time to meet with my president. During this time, we exchanged ideas and concerns. When a news flash occurred, I included my PTA president on my short list of people to call. For example, when I received notification that I was going to become a high school principal, I notified my middle school PTA president. I wanted her to be informed of all the important matters.

Also, include community leaders in special events and honor them in the presence of your students. By doing so, you will promote good citizenship and respect for others. One year, our student council honored the alumni who became elected public servants. We called the effort Great Leaders Who Walked the Halls of Our School. Through your quest to include community leaders as your valued stakeholders, you will develop a positive relationship with these key leaders by getting to know them and communicating your programs and needs to them.

POWER AND THE POWER OF THE PEN

Power is like money in the bank; don't withdraw all your power at once.

—S. W. Ingram, principal

WRITTEN COMMUNICATION

In chapter 12, we discussed verbal communication. Now, we will talk about written communication. The written word is the most powerful form of communication because it is everlasting. Be extremely careful about any written document you produce. Is the document accurate? Is it grammatically correct? Does it convey your intended message? Will you be proud of this document if it is printed in the newspaper? Would you be proud of the document if it is presented to the superintendent or board of education? Before you put a written reprimand into the hands of an employee, share this information with your superintendent to ensure his or her support prior to dissemination.

Letters and Memos

In spite of the exponential power of email, letters and memos are still important communication tools. Letters and memos are official documents that are mailed to people every day in order to solidify business contracts. In our school system, new employees are notified of their official hiring date with a mailed letter from the superintendent that signifies that the board of education approved the person's hiring. It further states the position for which the individual was hired and the effective dates of employment. Letters are sent to parents notifying them of serious disciplinary infractions that may result in a student's expulsion from the school. Letters and memos are important, official tools of business communication.

With this in mind, write letters and memos sparingly. If you send memos to your faculty and staff every day, they will probably become immune to these memos and not give them as much attention as they would if they only received a memo occasionally. Make sure you have an important reason to send a memo or email to your staff. Minimize these communications. By doing so, you will elevate the importance of your written communications and your staff will be more likely to read them. See appendix D for a sample memo.

Your Signature

Your signature is precious. Guard it. Do not authorize anyone to sign documents for you. If you create a PDF file with your signature, give it only to your secretary to use with your approval. All official letters and documents should be reviewed by you as principal and given your official seal of approval with your unique signature. Use a bold pen to proudly sign your name, because a fine pointed pen appears weak on a letter. I like to use a felt-tipped pen to sign my letters. Remember to sign applications for grants and annual reports in blue ink to signify an original signature for those receiving your documents.

Official Letter from the Principal

In chapter 6, we discussed how we can help others by encouraging them with an official letter of commendation. Use the official letter with the signature of the principal to acknowledge colossal achievements of your faculty, staff, and students. Look for additional ways to honor these people by nominating them for recognition through awards that are offered by your professional organizations, state department of education, or local PTA.

Email

Email is a double-edged sword. Be careful, my friend, when you use email. It is a dangerous tool because it is void of emotion and it can be forwarded to literally thousands of people with the touch of a finger. It can be difficult to comprehend one person's intended message at times because email contains none of the voice inflection and body language that accompanies verbal communications.

You will receive important, official emails from your supervisor, the state department of education, and your faculty and staff. You will receive emails from parents, students, friends, and members of the community. You will also receive silly joke emails and spam emails advertising products. With an effective email filter, these spam emails should be minimized. Try to answer emails within twenty-four hours. Do not get into the habit of checking your email every few minutes.

Only check your email three times a day; that is sufficient. Otherwise, email can become a distraction to your work productivity.

Remember when you answer emails, you are providing a written, official response from the principal's office. Do so prudently. If your answer is complicated and lengthy, you might consider simply calling the person instead of putting a lengthy response in an email. Be brief in your responses and do not show emotion or personal feelings. State the facts. Be careful! Your response may be forwarded to scores of people. There is no such thing as an informal response. Be grammatically correct, even in your emails. Personnel and student issues are best discussed verbally. If you are involved in a legal matter, you may be required to produce all emails related to the matter, so be cautious about what you say in an email. You may have to read it aloud in a court of law one day.

Be professional with your email. Neither read nor forward silly, sappy, or religious emails. Sending these types of emails to your faculty is unprofessional. In fact, receiving such emails may leave the impression that you have a lot of time to "play" in your office.

FACULTY MEETINGS AND AGENDAS

You, as principal, have the power to call faculty meetings at your school. When I became a middle school principal, my sister, Rhonda Anderton, gave me a piece of wise advice related to faculty meetings. Rhonda, a third-grade teacher, told me to control the length of faculty meetings, only call them when necessary, and respect the teachers by letting them know in advance when or if a faculty meeting will be held or canceled. I followed my sister's helpful advice through the years. I tried to hold faculty meetings only when necessary and I scheduled them in advance so the teachers could plan accordingly. Many of the teachers have to make arrangements to pick up children in the afternoon, so they appreciate the advance notice. I also told the teachers we would try to have faculty meetings end by 4:00 p.m. We usually could end the meeting in this forty-minute allotted time if we stayed with the agenda.

Speaking of agendas, always have an agenda for the faculty meeting. It will keep the teachers focused on the purpose of the meeting. There may be one teacher who likes to bring up subjects that are not on the agenda. If this happens, tell the teacher we can address this issue at the completion of the agenda if time allows or at the next faculty meeting. Everyone will appreciate staying on the agenda so that they can leave at a set time.

The written word is the most powerful form of communication because it is everlasting.

—Jan Irons Harris

DISCIPLINE

Be Fair, Firm, and Consistent

To thine own self be true, and it must follow, as the night the day, thou canst not then be false to any man.

—William Shakespeare

STUDENT HANDBOOK

In chapter 14, we talked about "sticking to the book" and the importance of communicating written expectations to students related to discipline. The best vehicle to communicate expectations is a student handbook. A student handbook should contain rules and guidelines for students. Consequences should also be listed after the infractions. All of the content should be, of course, based on board policy. It also contains practical information for conducting business, such as, How does one receive permission to be absent? It is nice if you can include a list of "who to see" if the students have questions. An example may be, "Who do you see if you want information about a scholarship?" Then list the counselor's name, office location, phone number, and email address. Or, "Who do you see if you have a question about athletics?" Then list the athletic director's name and information.

It is also helpful to put a school calendar in your student handbook. Principal Lane Hill includes a calendar in his school's student handbook; it shows school events and athletic schedules throughout the year. It even includes the dates for faculty meetings, along with testing dates and extracurricular events, such as pageants and the prom.

This student handbook should be ragged and worn by the end of the year due to its daily usage. I used my handbook in almost every student discipline conference I had as an assistant principal and later as a principal. It is helpful to begin parent/student conferences by turning to the page of the handbook that relates to the student's infraction and reading the section to the student or ask him/her to read it to you.

If a student is sent to your office because he was fighting, for example, refer to the student handbook and show the student the policy that states it is against board policy to fight at school. Point out sanctions listed in the policy for you to base your punishment upon in order to try to correct this inappropriate behavior. You will avoid trouble if you base *all* your decisions on the board policies that govern your school and district. This will also lead to consistency in handling problems from student to student. This is critical. Exceptions to the rules will be noted by others who will expect the same exception for their child when they get into trouble.

SAY WHAT YOU MEAN AND MEAN WHAT YOU SAY

Undertake not what you cannot perform, but be careful to keep your promise.

—George Washington, 1745

The admonition to "say what you mean and mean what you say" is good advice for parents, teachers, and administrators. Be clear with your directions and keep your promises. If you make a statement or rule, be prepared to enforce it. If you cannot or will not enforce the rule, then do not state the rule. For example, if the rule is that students must be on time to class, and the consequence will be a detention for students who are tardy, you must be prepared to enforce this rule. It is easy to enforce the rules with those who are continually in trouble, however, you must treat everyone the same. You must enforce the consequence or punishment for the student who is tardy, regardless of the student's background.

If you have one or more assistant principals, determine consequences together so that if one student is sent to the office for smoking cigarettes, he will receive the same punishment regardless of the administrator he sees. Make a list of consequences to guide you in your decision-making in the area of discipline. This will make life much simpler for all administrators because students will be treated the same way.

While you are disciplining the student, remember the saying, "Don't throw the baby out with the bath water." By this, I mean that students will make mistakes. Once they have been punished for the discipline infraction, start anew with the student. Do not discard the student because of one mistake. You can count on discipline issues to consume a large part of your day each day you serve as an administrator. This is especially true if you have a large student body. When you conference with students, give them the respect they deserve and speak to them with kindness and sincerity. Do not humiliate a student by correcting him or her in front of others. Treat students the same. Be fair, firm, and consistent in your actions.

Believe the best of your students and encourage them to do better the next time. Respect the students who are entrusted to your care. Have high expectations for them and treat them as you would want others to treat your own children. Do not believe every story given to you by your students. I have heard a lot of stories in my career. Remember that the student gave the teacher a reason to write a disciplinary referral. In general, believe the teacher and support the authority of teachers. At times, the teacher may be wrong but those will be the anomaly.

CAST NOT YOUR PEARLS BEFORE SWINE

I worked with Mr. Doug Styles for seven years while we were both serving as assistant principals at Grissom High School. I learned a number of valuable lessons from watching Mr. Styles—especially in the area of student discipline.

I remember one student who continued to make mistakes. I spent countless hours trying to conference with him and encourage him to conform to the expectations of the school. I refused to give up on this young man. One day, Mr. Styles told me to "cast not your pearls before swine." This advice comes from Matthew 7:6, where Jesus said, "Give not that which is holy unto the dogs, neither cast ye your pearls before swine, lest they trample them under their feet, and turn again and rend you." In other words, it is dumb to waste your time speaking to a person who will not hear your message. I think Mr. Styles was saying that I should put my energy into helping those students who wish to be helped.

WORKING WITH STUDENTS: HEARTBREAKING AND INSPIRING EXPERIENCES

As principal of your school, you are serving in a unique position, a multifaceted position where you are the disciplinarian, the counselor, and the encourager. This position will hurt your heart. I believe I heard and saw it all during the many years I served as a school administrator. I took a pregnant fourteen-year-old girl home when her mother was unable to come to the school and then had to tell the girl's mother that the student was pregnant. I was there when my student cried because his girlfriend had an abortion. Another young man asked me to call his father and tell him that he had a venereal disease because he was afraid to tell his father. I met with students who had addictions to alcohol and drugs, and with those who were in gangs and in satanic cults. I took one student, at his request, to a police investigator when he told me he left the scene of an accident. I took another student to tour the jail in the hope of changing his view of the world.

I have made many home and hospital visits, as well as an occasional jail visit. I counseled students who misbehaved to get attention from parents who were too busy to notice their indiscretions. I worked with the family when a student died from substance abuse. I helped a family whose son committed suicide. I worked with the family when an accident occurred and death claimed a young life. And, I tried my best to help students who lost mothers and fathers through death or divorce. These experiences broke my heart.

Serving as principal will also inspire you. I also worked with many brilliant minds and strong bodies that were determined to do something with their talents. Many of my former students are now mothers and fathers, teachers, doctors, lawyers, engineers, professional athletes, ministers, police officers, and entrepreneurs. Some are proudly serving in the military; others are acting on the Broadway stage or playing an instrument in the symphony. I worked with students who graduated from Harvard, Princeton, and the military academies.

As principal, you will see it all and learn about life in the process. It can break your heart and inspire you simultaneously. One of the fascinating parts about being an administrator is that every day brings new challenges.

He who ignores discipline comes to poverty and shame, but whoever heeds correction is honored.

—King Solomon in Proverbs 13:18 (NIV)

MODEL EFFECTIVE USE OF TWENTY-FIRST-CENTURY TECHNOLOGY

Employ your time in improving yourself by other men's writings so that you shall come easily by what others have labored hard for.

—Socrates

Young people are often referred to as technology natives whereas middle-aged people are referred to as technology immigrants. This is because students who are currently in high school grew up with technology whereas people in their forties were introduced to technology later in life. So, students today are generally more comfortable with technology than older people. I remember having my first computer in the early 1980s when I was twenty-something.

I know older people who choose to use technology and, then again, I know others who choose not to. One eighty-five-year-old lady I know does not own a computer and has no idea how to send email or browse the Internet. And yet, a retired teacher in her late eighties recently sent an email to one of the educators in our system. She seemed to be confident about using technology. Regardless of your age, continue to learn and grow in the ever-changing world of technology. By continual learning, we are able to function more efficiently in the changing world in which we live.

LEARN ABOUT TECHNOLOGY EACH DAY

One way to grow intellectually is to attend professional conferences. The last three years I have attended the National School Board Association's T+L (Technology plus Leaders) conference. This conference provided a holistic view of the global world in which we live. Our school system presented at this conference for two consecutive years. At the conference, opportunities for networking were abundant. By talking to others, you can learn much about technology. During these conversations, do not hesitate to ask questions when you do not understand a process or a term.

Talk to younger people and students about technology everywhere you go. For example, several administrators and I recently had the opportunity to hear Thomas Friedman speak at Auburn University about his bestselling book, *The World Is Flat* (a history of the twenty-first century discussing the globalization and "flattening" of our world due to the emergence of technology). One of the principals and I went to a local coffee shop in order to talk to college students. I observed students on their laptops in the coffee shop. We interviewed a couple of female students who told us about communicating with their professors via the Internet. By talking to these two students, I learned about their college life while simultaneously realizing we are going in the right direction with our technology efforts in our school system. My investment of time was well worth the effort.

Use technology while conducting business. Model confidence in this important area to those you supervise. For example, schedule meetings using Outlook. This is a simple, effective, professional manner in which to schedule conferences. Use a handheld communications and organization device, like a Blackberry. Do not be afraid to try new venues. By demonstrating curiosity and enthusiasm, you will encourage teachers to confidently explore new technology possibilities. Learning is a lifelong process.

As a superintendent, I enjoy creating my own weekly calendar and distributing it by email to all employees along with various stakeholders. This calendar is a great way to highlight all the great accomplishments that the various schools are achieving. I distributed a weekly calendar to faculty and staff when I served as principal as well (see appendix E for a sample weekly calendar). I am proud to model effective use of technology through communication in this manner on a regular basis.

I strive to learn one new skill each month or so. Recently I learned to download digital pictures from my camera and send them to a photo website where I can order photo prints. Make a list of skills you desire to learn or improve and go forward with your quest to master the skill through independent learning or through professional development opportunities. Do not wait for these skills to come to you. You must go after them in an aggressive manner. In doing so, you will be more efficient at work in the process.

20

PUBLIC RELATIONS, POLITICS, AND DECISION-MAKING

TELL YOUR STORY

When I became a high school principal, I began the practice of creating an annual report, or executive summary, that we distributed to our stakeholders. In my case, I used the phrase *executive summary* because our school was accredited by the Southern Association of Colleges and Schools, and one of the requirements of accreditation included the principal writing an executive summary every five years. I decided this summary needed to be written each year instead of every five years, so I committed to writing a summary on an annual basis. The annual report included highlights of the school year, demographic information, test scores, accomplishments such as state championships, and information about faculty and staff. It also included photos. Parents, teachers, students, and members of the community often expressed appreciation for these summaries, which highlighted all the good things going on in my high school.

Create an annual report that reflects your style of leadership. I will caution you that it takes a tremendous amount of time to prepare this document, but it will be well worth your time investment. You might want to create a committee to help you gather information for the report. After you create your annual report, proof it several times for grammatical errors. Ask an English teacher to edit it prior to publishing the report. Enlist the help of a graphic artist to ensure the result is attractive and professional.

Creating an annual report enables you to document important facts that can be referenced in future years. Through the years, we referenced information that was captured in the annual report on a number of occasions. It became an invaluable tool and a historical document. I no longer relied on my memory of when we were

state champions in a particular sport. I simply referenced my report to easily recall the date. I also had the information written in my Little Black Book. As superintendent, I continue to create an annual report because of the positive feedback about them that I received through the years.

You have a duty, as principal, to present information about your school in a professional manner. An annual report can be displayed on your school's website and
distributed when you speak to individuals and groups. It is also a helpful tool when
recruiting teachers and new students. Members of the real-estate association consistently requested copies of my annual report to help them as they promoted
houses in my school district. An example of one of my high school annual reports
can be found in appendix F.

You have a story to tell while you are in the principal's office. Tell it well. Your
story creates an image of your school for the people with whom you talk. Tell your
story. Document the highlights of each school year through the use of an annual
report. Share your story through a plethora of avenues such as mail, websites, and
through the local real-estate offices.

> *Do a good job. Do a good job. Do a good job. Tell everyone about it.*

> —Advice from my Vanderbilt professor, Dr. Bill Furtwengler

GET AN A+ ON PUBLIC SPEAKING OPPORTUNITIES

There will be myriad circumstances in which you will be called upon to "say a few
words." You will be invited to speak at banquets, awards ceremonies, and civic meetings about your school. There will be times at events when people will spontaneously
ask you to speak. Additionally, there will be numerous occasions when you will be
welcoming guests to the school and/or serving as the emcee for programs.

Here are a few general reminders when speaking in a public, formal arena:

- After you are introduced with your prepared biographical sketch (see the au-
  thor biography at the end of this book for an example), walk to the podium
  enthusiastically while displaying excellent posture. Walk with confidence.
- Smile.
- Pause for about 3–5 seconds before speaking.
- Get comfortable with the microphone. If you are taller or shorter than the
  previous speaker, adjust the microphone so you can stand tall while speaking.
- Do not slouch or fidget while at the podium.
- Do not jingle change in your pocket or put your hands in your pocket while
  speaking.
- Speak slowly to enunciate. Be articulate.
- Do not yell into the microphone. Speak at a normal volume.
- Think before you speak.
- Concentrate.

- Make eye contact with members of the audience.
- Strive to avoid having notes when delivering public speeches. My former minister, Larry Dill, taught me by example how to deliver speeches without using notes. He had two to three key points that he could remember and from which he could deliver his message. You can learn to deliver speeches without having notes in front of you—it just takes practice. It is more effective to talk directly to the audience rather than being attached to the podium and your notes during your delivery.

Welcome Ideas

If you are delivering an introduction or welcome to a program, begin by introducing yourself so that the honored guests will know who you are. Do not assume that everyone knows that you are the principal. Look at the audience and consider beginning the welcome with a quote such as:

Eleanor Roosevelt said, "Yesterday is history, tomorrow is a mystery. Today is a gift." As principal of this great school, I am pleased to share today with you as we celebrate the accomplishments of our students at the 2008 Grissom High School Awards Day Ceremony.

Another favorite of mine:

Helen Keller said, "Alone we can do so little, together we can do so much." Today, as we celebrate our students' accomplishments, we are mindful of parents, teachers, and others who helped our students achieve these accolades.

Formal Speeches

Prepare a practical speech in advance that you can use at a moment's notice. I did this as a principal and found it to be extremely effective. I call it my *Past, Present, and Future* speech, and I have used it multiple times during my career. Begin with a greeting and an overview of what you are going to share, such as:

Good Evening! On behalf of the faculty and students of Whitesburg Middle School, it is a pleasure for me to talk to you tonight about the past, the present, and the future of Whitesburg Middle School.

Convey your thoughts simply and with feeling. Begin by stating:

The Past. [*pause*] Whitesburg Middle School has a rich history of excellence since its founding in 1954.

Tell a few interesting tidbits about the school's *Past* such as different locations where the school was housed or how many students attended in 1954. Next, talk about the *Present*. Share the highlights from recent years such as state awards and/or test scores. People like to know how their school ranks in the state and nation. Give a couple of these comparisons. Statistics regarding the educational attainment of the faculty or the number of National Merit Finalists seem to be appreciated. Bring copies of your annual report for everyone (see an example of an annual report in appendix F). By distributing copies of your report, people have a visual aid to take home and share with others.

End your speech with an optimistic view of the *Future*. Talk about future predictions for growth or capital plans or new programs. Stay focused. If you are invited to speak for twenty minutes, be mindful of the time by placing your watch on the podium. Save a few minutes for questions at the conclusion of your speech. As questions are posed from the audience, repeat the question prior to answering it so everyone can hear the question in its entirety.

Final Reminders

Be simple. Tell the audience what you are going to say. Then, say it. Avoid the use of acronyms or fancy vocabulary. Use simple, easy to understand language during your speech. Close by summarizing your speech as a reminder of what you have shared with them.

> *To be simple is to be great.*
>
> —Ralph Waldo Emerson

POLITICS

Avoid politics at all costs. Do not put political signs in your yard or openly campaign for any local candidate. To do so will be a mistake. For, you see, you must work with whichever candidates are elected. If your candidate does not win, you will begin your relationship with this newly elected official in a negative manner.

Also, do not talk about politics or religion at school. You will alienate all the Democrats if they hear you blasting Democratic leaders or vice versa if you criticize Republican officials. This is not the time in your life to become actively involved in politics. Your employees should not know if you are a Republican or a Democrat because you should not discuss politics at work.

Do, however, be involved in communicating with the elected officials about issues related to education. Let those individuals know when you support a particular bill, for example. Do so with the blessing of your superintendent.

DECISION-MAKING

Make student and faculty decisions anonymously. For example, when an assistant principal comes to you for guidance with a discipline matter, do not ask for the student's name. Listen to the information and make a decision that is fair and consistent. Do not let the fact that a student has a prominent family change your decision. There will be a huge crowd watching you in these types of situations. Be careful to treat all students the same regardless of family background or economic status. We recently judged art entries for a billboard contest. We judged entries with no name on the front to ensure an objective selection process. Use the same technique while making decisions that affect your students.

Do not ever feel pushed to make an immediate decision—ever. If you need to sleep on a decision, do so. Talk to your mentor or supervisor for additional feedback, if necessary. Slow down when making important decisions and consider the consequences of your actions.

21

READ, STUDY, AND
TURN OFF THE TELEVISION

Learning is not a product of schooling but the lifelong attempt to acquire it.

—Albert Einstein

BE A LIFELONG LEARNER

One of the reasons Abraham Lincoln is my favorite president is because he was a self-made man. He was not born into wealth; his parents did not give him an Ivy League education. President Lincoln was a lifelong learner. He read incessantly and often read books aloud, which was said to have aggravated his law partner. He liked to read aloud because he said that it enabled him to capture the meaning of the book with two senses. He was able to see and to hear the book's message.

Abraham Lincoln credited his mother by saying, "All that I am or ever hope to be, I owe to my mother." I am sure there were many people who mentored Abraham Lincoln along his journey but the fundamental reason for his success, I believe, was because of his passion to learn. He was known to have walked miles to get a book he had not previously read.

It is my desire to also be a lifelong learner. Learning never stops. People who are lifelong learners lead rich, full lives until the day they die. They are avid readers who reap the benefits of learning physically and mentally. They are more alert and are able to ward off some illnesses by maintaining an active mind and a positive attitude about life. As I mentioned in the section on technology, an example of a lifelong learner is a retired teacher who, in her late eighties, became computer proficient. She emailed information to one of the teachers in our school system.

This inspired me! How many people do you know in their late eighties who are computer literate?

Read

Leaders are readers. What is the last book you read? What is the last educational journal you read? What is the last research you have read? What have you read for enjoyment? Reading is a fundamental part of our life as a principal. While you are in the principal's office, you will be bombarded with materials to read. You must decide what is worthy of reading. Begin by defining which journals you want to read on a regular basis. Most of your professional organizations will have journals and newsletters for you to read. As a principal, I enjoyed reading the *NASSP* (National Association of Secondary School Principals) *Bulletin*, for example. Once you decide which journals you wish to read, make time in your regular schedule to read them.

When I am reading professional journals, I often employ a reading strategy used through the Alabama Reading Initiative called "reading around the text" to help me assess the main point of the article without reading every word. The headings of each section tell the reader the content of the article. Peruse the entire article before beginning to read and form an opinion of the nature of the article before investing your precious time reading its contents.

As principal, occasionally I enjoyed taking my materials to the school library and reading in the presence of my students. Students are amazed when they see their teacher or principal in the library studying. I have had more than one student ask me, "What are you doing here, Dr. Harris?" I enjoy telling them that I am reading and studying. Also, make it easy to read. Have materials to read in your car so that when you are waiting in line at the bank, you can glance at a page of a report. Have reading materials beside your bed and next to your chair. Leave the newspaper and magazines on the kitchen table or island so that your family can read while eating breakfast.

I enjoy listening to books on tape in my car when I travel. You can use an MP3 player or iPod to listen to audio versions of books while exercising or traveling. Be careful to not have the volume too high so as to damage your hearing.

Read aloud to others from time to time. Enjoy reading! Read to your family at night and let them read to you instead of watching television. Read children's books and classics at night. Read the Bible and learn timeless skills for success from this bestselling book of all time.

In my journal, I record books that I read. I enjoy reviewing the list from time to time. This list inspires me to do further reading on topics of interest. I also feel like I have accomplished a lot when I see the record of books I have read on the pages of my journal.

Study

Study just as you did in college. As principal, you must stay abreast of new developments by reading and studying and attending professional growth opportunities.

As you arrange your daily and weekly schedule, protect time for reading and studying each day. I tell my students to use the "10 times the grade you are in" rule to determine a reasonable amount of time to study each night. For example, it would be reasonable for a sixth grader to study 60 minutes each night (10 × 6 = 60 minutes). What is a reasonable amount for you, as principal, to study each day? You might start by striving to read and study an hour each day. It is my experience that this will be difficult for you to achieve. Whether you peruse current events or study with great intensity, make time to read and study each day.

Become an Expert

As you read and study, you will naturally develop areas of interest. For example, I am interested in leadership, communication, technology, character education, art, and reading. I gravitate toward information on these topics. Because of this personal interest, I collect information and am knowledgeable about these topics. You will become "an expert" on a topic of interest if you study and read about it regularly.

Principal Elton Bouldin did just that. He reads and studies everything he can find about the No Child Left Behind Act. As a result, he has become an expert on the subject of student assessment at the state and local level.

When you are knowledgeable about a topic, write an article about the topic and submit it for publication in a professional journal. Create a speech on a topic you study and be ready to discuss it. Volunteer to present this information to your students or at a local or state professional development event. I created a workshop called Math Curriculum Triangulation when I was a middle school principal. I presented it for teachers in our school system and taught them to align their local curriculum to state and national standards. I also have presented lectures about Abraham Lincoln to history classes. Remember, you cannot know everything about every topic but you can be an "expert" on a few topics of interests.

> *The learning and knowledge that we have, is, at the most, but little compared with that of which we are ignorant.*
>
> —Plato

TURN OFF THE TELEVISION

According to the facts presented by Nielson in 2006 at www.turntvoff.org, the average American home has the television on eight hours a day, and the average adult watches television four hours and thirty-five minutes a day! It is easy to fill the silence in your home with television noise. When my husband was young, his father died when he was forty years old from a massive heart attack. His mother hated the quiet in the house and so she liked to have the television on at a loud volume when she was home. When we married, Wholey told me he did not like to come home to a loud television when he walked through the doors. Consequently, we never got into a habit on turning on the television when we got home in the afternoon.

Turning the television on immediately upon waking or walking in the house is a habit that can be easily formed. Before you habitually turn on the television and begin mindless surfing, ask yourself how you want to spend your evening. What can you do that would parallel your mission and values or inspire you to be a better person? Only turn on the television when you have a specific purpose, such as watching the news or watching a favorite show. When the show ends, turn off the television. Enjoy the quiet or listen to your favorite music. Use this time to read or talk to family members.

I challenge you to turn off the television for an extended period. Enjoy a technology fast. I did this when I was a middle school principal and I encouraged my students to do the same. I did not watch television for more than a month. It was an amazing experience! I felt as though I had unlimited time. I had time to take a walk, read, visit, write, study, exercise, and clean. From this experience I developed my quote, "Read, study, and turn off the television." I still do not watch a lot of television and I am proud of this fact. If someone told me I would win a prize if I could name which shows come on each night, I would not be able to answer this question and I am fine with this. I do not find many television shows today that are uplifting and thought-provoking. When I have the television on, I mostly find violence and titillating plots. I do not find this to be relaxing for me. I do enjoy the History channel and other informational channels.

When I turn off the television and have time to read or write, I enjoy listening to classical music. I have an eclectic musical taste and like to listen to Christian, pop, and country music. We enjoy going to the symphony or musical concerts from time to time. Music is a beautiful gift to mankind. It can be personally tailored to your individual preferences. An MP3 player is an excellent tool to customize your musical tastes. I thoroughly enjoy using my iPod when I am writing, taking a walk, or traveling on a plane.

Often, at my home, we will simply turn on the radio at night. It is an old-fashioned ritual that my husband and I enjoy immensely. We enjoy listening to public radio as well as other radio stations from time to time. It is relaxing and fun to recall a particular song that we have not heard in years.

Silence is golden. Experiment with silence. I challenge you to have one night or even one hour in complete silence—no television, no radio or music, and no talking. It will be difficult, but you may be able to clear your mind and focus completely during this activity, especially with practice. I learned a valuable lesson about silence one night at a church service when our minister asked everyone to leave the sanctuary in silence and remain silent all the way to your car. This gift of silence gave me peace and it was refreshing to walk without conversation or noise.

Instead of having blaring noise, think about what you allow to enter into your mind and control it. I tell my students to guard their minds. I use the analogy of early civilizations existing with gates surrounding the perimeter of the city. Usually, men guarded the entrances to the city, and the city had massive doors that prevented intruders from entering the city uninvited. Just as the people guarded their city with their lives, we must guard our minds. Our mind is the greatest gift we have and we must protect and nurture it continually.

Guard your mind. Control what enters through the gate. If you find an individual to be a "prophet of doom" and you leave feeling deflated and depressed after a conversation with this individual, avoid this person and do not interact with him or her unless it's unavoidable. If you find the news report to be alarming and negative, do not watch it every morning and night. Instead, read the headlines on the Internet news site of your choice. Do not watch movies or read books that are upsetting. Control what enters your mind each day. Guard your mind. Be like the guard at the gate and ask if the person or idea seeking entrance needs to enter into your city walls.

An investment in knowledge always pays the best interest.

—Benjamin Franklin

SUMMARY OF PART III
KEYS FOR INTELLECTUAL BALANCE

1. Be professional at all times. Understand the scope of your responsibility as principal. Understand the organizational chart of your school system. Know the chain of command and communicate in this manner.
2. Stick to the book. Use board policy to ground every decision you make as principal. Be knowledgeable about state and federal laws that affect school administration.
3. Create a student handbook and communicate its contents to all of your students and parents. Have students and parents sign a document acknowledging receipt of this important guide that provides an operational foundation for your school.
4. Create plans for every imaginable situation. Some of these plans are mandated by your state department of education while others will be plans you create to promote an awareness of possible situations that could occur during your tenure as principal.
5. Build your winning team by carefully selecting each team member. Thoroughly review resumes and application packets. Take time to have an in-depth interview with each potential candidate, and do not forget to check references.
6. Mentor new teachers and staff by assigning an official mentor to them. Also, mentor these employees yourself through conversations, meetings, observations, and encouragement.
7. Improve employees' performance through communication of high expectations and accountability.
8. Build morale in your school by establishing relationships, initiating times of fellowship, and using school spirit items such as t-shirts.

9. Remember that the written word is the most powerful form of communication because it is everlasting. Be careful about what you put in writing! Make sure the content is accurate. Make sure it is grammatically correct. Visualize this document on the front page of your newspaper; it could be printed there one day. Be proud of your documents.

10. Be fair, firm, and consistent in matters of discipline and employee supervision. Treat all people with whom you interact with kindness and respect. Refer to your board and student handbooks often.

11. Model effective use of twenty-first-century technology. Be a lifelong learner.

12. Work to communicate your story to all stakeholders through public speaking, websites, and annual reports. Speak about your school with enthusiasm and confidence.

13. Avoid politics. Period.

14. Read, study, and turn off the television!

IV

EMOTIONAL BALANCE

A few of the descriptors of the emotional domain include self-esteem, worry, stress, forgiveness, social events, and relationships. Life in the principal's office can be like a roller-coaster ride. It will definitely have its ups and downs. Maintain a calm demeanor at all times—regardless of how stressful any situation may be. Students and teachers are looking for you to set the tone for all situations that arise. Assure others that you are in control by being calm and levelheaded. In other words, it is imperative that you maintain control of your emotions.

> *All loving emotions, like plants, shoot up most rapidly in the tempestuous atmosphere of life.*
>
> —Richter in *Dictionary of Thoughts* (1877)

22

TEFLON MENTALITY AND WALNUTS

TEFLON MENTALITY

It's not about you.

My husband Wholey likes a scrambled egg sandwich for breakfast at times. I enjoy preparing these sandwiches for him. I use a favorite Teflon-coated frying pan to cook the eggs. I like to use this pan because it is easy to get the eggs out of the pan and onto the plate; the eggs simply slide out of the pan because of the Teflon coating. A secondary reason to use this pan involves cleanup. It only takes a few seconds to wash this pan because there is no residue on the Teflon coating.

Life happens. Students misbehave. Parents will be upset. Employees do make mistakes. There may be scandals. You, as the principal, will have to sort it all out. Dealing with the issue is like putting the eggs into the Teflon pan to cook. You are like the pan. The problem comes to you and you must deal with it. But, in the end, it is released. It is not about you. Do not absorb the issue. Let it slip away like the scrambled eggs slide out of the pan.

Once, while dealing with a discipline issue, a parent was hurling questions at me in an elevated voice while pointing her finger at me. I interrupted her ranting and told her we were going to start this conference over. I told her that I was not on trial and that I would not be spoken to in this manner. I told her I did not put the knife into her daughter's backpack; her daughter made the decision to bring the weapon to school. I explained that I was simply the person dealing with this issue. After this explanation, the woman apologized, relaxed a bit, and starting talking in a normal tone of voice.

Do not allow yourself to be mistreated—ever. Do not absorb problems. Display Teflon mentality. By doing so, you will be able to handle problems in an

Recipe: Wholey's Scrambled Egg Sandwich

Place an empty glass in the freezer to chill it.

Whisk 3 eggs together in a large bowl. Add 1/4 cup shredded cheese. Add 1/4 cup of milk and whisk all ingredients together. Heat a Teflon-coated frying pan and put a small amount of olive oil in the pan. Pour egg mixture into the frying pan and add salt and fresh ground pepper while the eggs are cooking. While the eggs cook, toast whole wheat bread. Once the eggs are cooked, let them slide out of the pan onto the freshly toasted bread. Slice the egg sandwich in half. Serve with fresh fruit. (Wholey's favorite fruits are blackberries and strawberries). Remove the chilled glass from the freezer and fill it with milk.

Enjoy!

unemotional manner. You will be calm and in control because you maintain Teflon mentality.

BE A WALNUT INSTEAD OF A GRAPE

May I be candid? Are you a grape or a walnut? Let me explain.

Are you sensitive? Do your feelings get hurt easily? Do you take the infrequent emotional outbursts by parents and students personally? Do you replay incidents over and over and over again in your mind? Do you become defensive when people criticize your actions? If you answered *yes* to these questions, you must be a grape. You have thin skin like a grape. You let circumstances affect you personally.

Are you strong? Do you realize that people have a right to state their own opinion? Do you realize that, at times, people become upset and say irrational things while emotional? Do you accept criticism and objectively look at situations to see if you can improve? Do you understand that challenges will happen at your school and you, as the principal, will handle the situation and leave it at school when you go home at the end of the day? If you answered *yes* to these questions, then you must be a walnut.

In a class for aspiring administrators, I displayed two bowls on the conference table. One bowl contained grapes; another contained walnuts. I instructed these future principals to pass a grape and a walnut around the table so that each person could hold them. During this exercise, I explained my analogy of grapes and walnuts to the class. Months later, one of the aspiring administrators told me that she keeps a walnut on her desk to remind her to be strong and not take situations personally.

Be a walnut; be strong. Be able to listen to criticism without letting it affect you personally. For example, I recall teachers complaining when we had an assembly and I had to create a schedule for the remainder of the day. There was no way I could please every teacher. The P.E. teachers wanted to assume the normal schedule so they could have enough time in the remaining classes for students to dress out and participate. However, the academic teachers wanted abbreviated classes because they preferred to keep their classes on the same schedule in the curriculum. They preferred meeting fifteen minutes with each class rather than miss a class. My point is that with either schedule I chose, I knew that someone would be unhappy. In the end, I prepared a schedule that was in the best interest of the students.

Be prepared for the unexpected. Acknowledge that the unusual may occur. For example, while I was a principal, I experienced these events: a homeless person sleeping in the building, animals getting in the building, a ceiling falling in, and an employee being arrested. You never know what will happen on any given day. Keep a sense of humor about it all and do not feel as though you can control these events. You cannot control the weather or acts of nature. You cannot control other people. Realize this fundamental truth and be prepared for the unexpected.

Deal with issues. Make decisions. Be tough like a walnut, not thin-skinned like a grape. Lead with confidence and do not let issues easily seep through your skin and get to you personally. Make all decisions based on the best interest of the students.

It is not the critic who counts: not the man who points out how the strong man stumbles or where the doer of deeds could have done better. The credit belongs to the man who is actually in the arena, whose face is marred by dust and sweat and blood, who strives valiantly, who errs and comes up short again and again, because there is no effort without error or shortcoming, but who knows the great enthusiasms, the great devotions, who spends himself for a worthy cause; who, at the best, knows, in the end, the triumph of high achievement, and who, at the worst, if he fails, at least he fails while daring greatly, so that his place shall never be with those cold and timid souls who knew neither victory nor defeat.

—Theodore Roosevelt

DON'T LET THE TURKEYS GET YOU DOWN

George Herbert Walker Bush served as the forty-first President of the United States from 1989 to 1993. When he arrived at the White House to begin his tenure as president, the outgoing president, Ronald Reagan, gave him some words of advice: "Don't let the turkeys get you down." President Bush shared this personal story at President Reagan's funeral.

When President Bush's son, George W. Bush, was running for president of the United States in 2000, he was interviewed by Oprah Winfrey on her talk show. She asked him if he cared what people thought about him. With a boyish grin, he told her that he cared what 51 percent of the people thought of him! The audience exploded with laughter.

Presidents are continually criticized because of their policies, actions, and positions. When President Bill Clinton was in office, some individuals even criticized what he ate! The president must remain focused and calm. The president must keep the best interest of our country as the top priority at all times. Imagine what our great country would be like if our president incessantly focused on the negative.

During your time in the principal's office, you will meet people who support you. You will meet people who disagree with you and do not support you. You will meet people who will pretend to be your friend until you make a decision that they do not like. You will work with dedicated students; you will work with students who will likely go to prison one day. In order to be successful, you must remain optimistic and focused on your mission and goals (see chapter 1 for more information on determining your mission).

Speaking of people who pretend to be your friends, remember that there are no friends like old friends. Do not become personal friends with those you supervise even though some will seek your personal time and attention. It is fine to go to an occasional open house or holiday party, but it is best if you do not become personal friends with your staff members. Keep your distance and remain the principal—not someone's personal buddy. You will be wise to keep your distance; by doing so you will not have to deal with the perception that you are showing favoritism toward an employee. Also, if that employee needs to be corrected, you might find it difficult to do so if you are personal friends. Stay focused on your job—not on social events.

One of the ways I stay positively focused is by periodically writing in my journal and revisiting my goals in life. I strive to control the thoughts I allow to develop in my mind. I do not allow negative thoughts to inhabit my mind. I remember, years ago, when I was in my administrative infancy, I confessed to my father, Bobby Irons, that I kept thinking about an issue over which I had no control. He told me to remember that I have bigger fish to fry when the small matters try to dominate my thoughts. I have held this wise advice close to my heart and mind through the years while in the principal's office. This metaphor captures my advice perfectly: I know it is difficult to not replay incidents over and over in your mind, but you *can* control your thoughts with discipline.

Because I am a collector of quotes, I often write inspirational thoughts on my bathroom mirror with a dry-erase marker. I remember writing President Reagan's advice, "Don't let the turkeys get you down!" on my dad's bathroom mirror when he was first elected as mayor. He left this wise advice on his mirror for a long time.

Simply realize this: There are negative people and there are positive people. There are challenges in all situations. Focus on the positive. See the good in every situation. Do not spend the majority of your time dwelling on the negative. Put your energy into positive efforts. Deal with problems but don't let them consume all your time and energy.

Don't let the turkeys get you down.

—Ronald Reagan

23

DELEGATE AND LEARN TO SAY NO

DELEGATE

Consider this analogy: Think about a favorite glass that you use on a consistent basis. I am thinking of a pretty crystal glass that belonged to my mother-in-law. Often, when I cook supper, I will use this glass to hold tea or water. The glass will hold approximately eight ounces of liquid. I usually must refill the glasses during the course of the meal because the glass will only hold this limited amount of liquid.

Now, consider your energy for a moment. We begin each day with a certain amount of energy, and this is the amount we are able to use for the duration of each day's events. Certainly, there are times that you may use more or less energy, but on a general basis, you have this level amount of energy each day. Guard your energy. If you use too much of your energy at work, then you will be exhausted when you come home in the afternoon. I have experienced this sensation on many occasions. If you use too much of your energy at home in the morning, you will be tired when you walk in the door of the principal's office. If you consistently deplete your energy reserves before completing your day at work, you will feel stress and have a sense of "never catching up" at work. This can negatively affect your emotional well-being.

The key to maintaining balance with your energy is to learn how to delegate. As principal, you cannot do it all, even though, if you are like me, often you will prefer to do tasks yourself rather than rely on others. If you insist on doing all tasks yourself, you will burnout quickly because this job requires a tremendous amount of energy and attention; one person cannot do it all.

Serving effectively as principal requires a team approach to getting the job done each day. Use this team approach and start delegating as soon as you have a solid knowledge of the people with whom you work. If you have an assistant principal, you will delegate a number of tasks to this individual. In a large school such as Grissom High School, which had more than 2,300 students when I served as an assistant principal, there were three assistant principals. Each assistant principal had specific duties. For example, one assistant was responsible for overseeing the facility and athletics; another was responsible for curriculum; another was responsible for student services, including guidance and attendance. All assistants shared overseeing discipline as well as completing faculty and staff evaluations.

Once you determine which tasks will be delegated to others, clearly communicate your expectations to the person charged with the responsibility of getting the work done. Then, follow-up in a few days to make sure the task was completed to your level of satisfaction. You will find that, in most cases, people will rise to the level of expectation. People will disappoint you at times, but it has been my experience that most individuals working in schools are highly conscientious educators who are dependable and loyal.

Guide those to whom you delegate and encourage them by communicating your satisfaction with their efforts. Gently correct if the end results are not to your satisfaction. By appropriately delegating the tasks that others can do, you will be able to focus on the tasks that *you need to do* such as meeting with people, preparing speeches for events, writing letters, attending meetings, or preparing agendas for programs or meetings. If you clearly understand your role in the organization, then it will be easier to delegate.

For example, if you are a high school principal who has one or more assistant principals, you probably should not spend your time working with students who are tardy or misbehave. For minor student discipline issues, the principal does not need to be spending time and energy overseeing these types of issues. However, it is important that the principal be available to meet with parents when they have a concern. Otherwise, the parents may elevate their concern to the superintendent. It is the principal's job to take care of all matters at the school. Period. As a principal, I considered it a failure when issues from my school ended up at the central office. If you do your job, these referrals to a higher level will be few and far between.

LEARN TO SAY NO

If you learn how to say no, you will have more time for the important matters that you will face in the principal's office. In choosing which events to attend and participate in, remember that you will be courted when you arrive in the principal's office. Realize that you, personally, did not suddenly become the most popular person in town. People will want you to be part of their group because of your position. Vendors will invite you to lunch, and groups and individuals will seek your friendship and involvement. Once you determine your mission (see chapter 1 for more information on determining your mission), you will be able to decide if a particular invitation is in concert with your goals. Then, it will be easier for you to determine if you need to participate in a particular event.

A particular example comes to mind. I recall being asked to judge an essay contest for a business in the community. I am more than happy to do my part with community endeavors and, without a great deal of thought, I agreed to do the judging. This was a task that would take me several hours to complete. It was not necessary for me, as principal, to do this task. The judge would remain anonymous, but there was not a correlation between my area of expertise and the contest requirements. I remember I set the task aside because I was busy. Life is always busy in the principal's office.

When the contest judging deadline approached, I realized I needed to fulfill my obligation. I took the papers with me to a professional conference and spent a couple of nights in my room reading and judging the entries. This experience made me realize that my energy is precious. My time is precious. So is yours. Decide what is unrelated to your mission in life and refuse to waste time in the areas unrelated to your goals. The next year, I was asked to judge the entries again, but I politely declined the invitation. Do not let yourself become immersed in tasks and obligations that are unrelated to your job or that are unimportant. Spread the responsibility. Let others participate.

By learning to delegate and say no, you will be in control of your energy. Distribute your energy in a balanced manner with thoughtful consideration.

You and these people who come to you will only wear yourselves out. The work is too heavy for you; you cannot handle it alone. Listen now to me and I will give you some advice . . . select capable men from all the people . . . and appoint them as officials. . . . That will make your load lighter, because they will share it with you. If you do this and God so commands, you will be able to stand the strain, and all these people will go home satisfied.

—Jethro, speaking to his son-in-law
Moses in Exodus 18:18–23 (NIV)

(24)

CREATE INSPIRING AND PRODUCTIVE LEARNING ENVIRONMENTS

What inspires you? Where is your favorite place in your house? City? State? Country? World? Think about why this place is your favorite place. One of my favorite places in the United States is the Library of Congress located in Washington, D.C. While visiting in Washington, my husband and I toured the nation's library and obtained a library card. I found the Library of Congress to be most inspiring for several reasons. First, it is a beautifully designed building. Second, thought-provoking and attractive quotes can be found above the doorways. Third, it is peaceful within the walls of this magnificent facility. People inside the library talk in hushed tones. There is order; there are beautiful, empty tables waiting for people to sit down and use while reading and absorbing information or, perhaps, creating written documents.

I try to replicate this environment at home and work when I am striving to produce my best work. I cannot work productively in the midst of chaos. I like to have silence or listen to classical music while I am working. My idyllic vision of an inspiring work environment may not be attainable for those with small children at home. Recently I read a story about a family with septuplets. I imagine it must be quite difficult for this stay-at-home mother to find time and physical space to work. I can visualize the little children's toys and shoes throughout the house. I assume this "supermom" would do her mental work after the children have gone to bed in order to find a time free from distractions. You may also find this inspiring work time after everyone has gone to bed.

I am not advocating doing a lot of work at home. When I use the word "work," I am referring to times of creativity and learning for joy. I encourage you to do your work at the office. Have a place that is inspiring and productive at home for personal pursuits, and another such place in your office.

I have a number of favorite places to work in my house. I rotate my workspaces from time to time. I like to work at my dining room table where I have space to spread out my documents and write. I also enjoy using an antique farm table in my family room, and I frequently use the island in my kitchen to work upon while either sitting on the bar stool or standing. As principal, consider your needs for an inspiring and productive work environment while also considering the needs of your students.

SUGGESTED IMPROVEMENTS TO YOUR WORKSPACE

Create an inspiring and productive work environment for you and your students. I offer a few suggestions below that might help:

1. Clean your desk regularly. Remove items from your desk, and clean the surface before beginning a new project. Discard clutter and remove unneeded paperwork on your desk. Read mail and handle papers only once. File, act, delegate, or discard.
2. Clean out your drawers two or three times a year to help you be aware of the contents of each drawer. Maintain supplies that are needed on a daily basis such as staples, tape, paperclips, and scissors. Keep glass cleaner, furniture polish, a dust cloth, and paper towels together in a basket in your closet to assist you in cleaning your work space as needed. A furniture touch-up pen for scratches is also nice to have in order to keep your furniture looking new.
3. Line the drawers of your desk with maps. Each time you open the drawer you will see the map and it will remind you that it is your responsibility as principal to determine the best path into the future for your school. Measure the size of each drawer, cut the map to fit and use two-sided tape to hold the map drawer liner to the bottom of the drawer.
4. Have an artifact on your desk created by a student. I currently have a precious drawing on my desk. It was created by an elementary student; it says, "Read and relax." Looking at this drawing keeps my students foremost in my mind as I work each day. As I make one decision at a time throughout the day, I think about the precious drawing and my students. Is my current decision in their best interest?
5. Display an updated photo of your family on your desk so that you can gaze upon it and be reminded of the people who love you most. Looking at this photo will bring you joy during the day.
6. Fill a pencil holder with pens that work well along with a few freshly sharpened pencils. I keep new pencils available to give to students when they come to visit. Keep extra pencils to reward students. Regardless of our age, it is fun to receive a new pencil with school colors and name imprinted upon it.
7. Keep a stack of notepads available in a drawer so that when you need paper, you do not have to start a scavenger hunt to locate a notepad.

8. Have an attractive leather binder readily available with your university logo or your school or system logo on it. You will use this binder over and over again as you attend meetings and visit classrooms. You can use it also to transport important documents to central office.
9. Store bottled water nearby so you will have it when you need it.
10. Keep a beautiful mug or cup and saucer to use when drinking tea, coffee, or water.
11. Remove and rotate items that clutter your office. Do not display numerous items from years ago such as multiple photos from your previous job. Keep only a few mementos from the past in your office. Box these past mementos and keep current artifacts like photos of your current students and faculty on display. You will receive a multitude of knickknacks from students through the years. Keep them in a storage box and extract them from time to time in order to waltz them around your office. By rotating these displays, you will keep your office fresh and alive. Do not weigh it down by covering every square inch with gifts from the past. Leave some space unoccupied for the future.
12. Organize the documents in your office using color. I once enlisted the help of a professional organizer, Kathryn Daniel, to help me manage the massive amount of information that flows into my office; she recommended organizing important information by color. My assistant, Jackie Joiner, uses colored folders to organize information. For example, my blue folder is a signature folder, the red folder contains important documents to read, and the green folder holds newsletters and journals. Jackie and I use plastic covered black binders with different paper colors to identify each binder. These identifying sheets are inserted behind the plastic sleeve so that I can find documents with ease. Kathryn recommended that I use one color of paper for our system's documents, another for state documents, and a third for federal papers.
13. Make it a priority to have excellent lighting over your desk or table. Purchase a lamp for your desk to provide additional light.
14. Invest in a comfortable chair. Your back will be glad that you did so. Adjust it so that your feet touch the floor and also your arms and hands are at the proper height to use your computer or sign documents.
15. Consider having an alternate surface that enables you to stand while working. At times, I will simply stand at the counter in the main office to sign or review documents or read mail. I have a podium in my office that I frequently use while reading documents or signing documents. Principal Lane Hill suggested the use of a podium to me. I find it to be quite effective because I do not like to sit excessively. When I was a middle school principal, we remodeled the front office and included an island in the center of the office space. It was at counter height and was used constantly by all who worked in the office. It was extremely efficient to sort papers or work at this location.

16. Consider holding walking meetings from time to time. Instead of sitting at a table for thirty minutes, take a walk and talk about your business in the process.

THE SCHOOL ENVIRONMENT

Make sure that your school reflects a creative and productive learning environment for your students. Principal Tricia Culpepper uses fresh colors and geometric designs to help create inspiring learning environments for her staff and students. She searches for creative, inexpensive ways to make spaces more functional. For example, in her conference room she has a metal chair rail with magnets to display important charts. Tricia's primary school hallways are adorned with student artwork as well as enlargements of the covers of current children's books. She also displays these inviting books in her office to encourage others to read and explore.

Maintain attractive displays of students' work in your school and keep the building clean at all times. Insist that teachers keep their rooms neat, attractive, and free from clutter. Create inspiring and productive learning environments for your students and staff.

> *Far away there in the sunshine are my highest aspirations. I may not reach them, but I can look up and see their beauty, believe in them, and try to follow where they lead.*
>
> —Louisa May Alcott

25

FORGIVENESS AND
SERVICE TO OTHERS

People ask me what advice I have for a married couple struggling in their relationship. I always answer: pray and forgive. And to young people from violent homes, I say pray and forgive. And again even to the single mother with no family support: pray and forgive.

—Mother Teresa

FORGIVENESS

Because life is not perfect, people will disappoint you. During the time you serve in the principal's office, people—including you—will make mistakes. Feelings will be hurt. A person's true character is revealed when a person makes a mistake and is corrected, or when a person is injured emotionally by another person. When life is rosy and full of sunshine, it is easy to be pleasant and professional. However, all days will not be rosy. There will be days when apologies need to be made and accepted.

It amazes me that there are individuals who simply will not apologize. It also amazes me that some people will not forgive others. Instead, they hate the person for the rest of their lives! One example of this refusal to forgive can be found in Shakespeare's play, *Romeo and Juliet*. The parents of these young lovers hated each other. Hence, Romeo and Juliet were forbidden to marry.

Conversely, in Victor Hugo's book, *Les Misérables*, we learn about the hero, Jean Valjean, who was the recipient of forgiveness. A priest forgave him after he stole silver candlesticks from this man of God. Instead of turning Jean Valjean over to the police, the priest told the police he had given Jean Valjean the silver candlesticks and then gave Jean more silver, explaining that he left the best gift of all. This forgiveness coupled with the gift of silver changed Jean Valjean's life forever. His life was changed for good because the priest forgave him.

If a teacher makes an inappropriate comment to a student, he or she should apologize in order to seek forgiveness. Students should apologize to each other when they have a squabble. Apologies are healing. However, you cannot force people to apologize—but you can encourage it. You can only control your actions and your reaction to others.

Practice the art of forgiveness each day you live. Even if an individual does not request forgiveness from you, forgive anyway. If you are holding any type of grudge against another person, forgive him or her. Forgive students when they make mistakes and have to be disciplined. Forgive others when they hurt you with their words or actions.

During your tenure as principal, you will have a few employees who may disagree with your decisions. You cannot please everyone. Do not make the mistake of believing that you can. When these few individuals make critical comments about your decisions, others will tell you about it. This is human nature. Do not approach the employee about the comment—simply forgive the person and move on, however difficult it may be. Do not harbor ill will toward the individual.

Wouldn't it be great if we could simply forgive others and erase the mistakes we make on a daily basis? What if we could erase the indiscretion from our memory after it occurred like a student erases mistakes with the eraser on his pencil while doing math homework? In order to be successful as a principal, you must learn to forgive others.

In the Jewish faith, forgiveness is an annual ritual celebrated during Yom Kippur. At this time, forgiveness is given and the people start anew. How wonderful! Forgiveness is a practice we should employ on a daily basis. We would live in a better world if we could forgive all wrongs at least once a year and start the year off with a clean slate in all of our relationships. You can have this erased, clean-slate feeling by practicing forgiveness on a daily basis. Forgive others and forgive yourself. And do not hesitate to ask others to forgive you if you offend them.

> . . . *Forgive, and you will be forgiven.*

> —Luke 6:37 (NIV)

SERVICE TO OTHERS

Life's most urgent question is: What are you doing for others?

—Dr. Martin Luther King Jr.

In order to be emotionally strong, we need to look outside of ourselves and search for ways to help others. We need to keep this ideal in front of our students, as well. Two of the people I admire because of their service to others are Nobel Peace

Prize winners Martin Luther King Jr. and President Jimmy Carter. Dr. King, when he received the Nobel Peace Prize, did not accept the approximately $50,000 in prize money; instead he gave it to further the civil rights movement. He gave his life to make others' lives better.

President Carter is an inspirational man due to his dedicated service to others. Through the years, he volunteered with Habitat for Humanity. He founded the Carter Center, a philanthropic center established to improve the lives of others. Through his center, he is leading the effort to eradicate river blindness and help alleviate the suffering caused by the Guinea worm.

Both of these men are amazing role models for all of us. Similarly, I will never forget my professor, Dr. Joseph Murphy, hosting brown-bag lunches while I was in graduate school. I am certain he had an abundance of items on his to-do list. However, he made time to help us learn practical skills like how to publish an article in an educational journal. He cared about us and took time away from his busy schedule to mentor us and teach us in innovative, helpful ways.

Emotionally strong people are often actively looking for ways to encourage and help others. During the time you serve in the principal's office, encourage your staff and students to deny our narcissistic tendencies and look for ways to constantly help others. In other words, do your job and look for one way, at least, that you can help others.

Do all the good you can,
By all the means you can,
In all the ways you can,
In all the places you can,
At all the times you can,
To all the people you can,
As long as ever you can.

—John Wesley

26

STRESS, 24/7 RESPONSIBILITY, AND THANKFULNESS

There is no doubt that serving as a principal is a stressful job. You are expected to remember large amounts of information including knowing all of the faculty and staff members along with your students. You are responsible for the security of your building. You will receive the phone call if someone breaks into the school or if the fire alarm sounds in the middle of the night. You will receive the sad call when one of your students or employees dies or is injured.

When a football player was injured at the game and had to be taken to the emergency room, I wanted to be there. I wanted to show my respect to the parents of my student who was killed in a rollerblading accident. I visited a young girl in the hospital who had lost her mother in a car wreck but fortunately the girl and her father survived the terrible accident. I wanted to try to do what I could to console them in this terrible time in their lives and to just let them know I would do whatever I could to make things easier for the little girl. I wanted to be there for the family when one of our employees committed suicide shortly after she lost her only child in a tragic accident. These types of tragedies led to the most difficult visits I ever made. I experienced all of these situations and, at times, felt like a minister.

Each of these situations I described was stressful. Know that these situations can happen at any time in your life as a principal and be prepared to handle the difficult situations. You will be the person who will be expected to respond as the head of the school to these tragic situations. How do you manage being on call 24 hours a day, 7 days a week, and 365 days a year? I found that even when I was away on vacation, I would receive a call when one of these events occurred. Each principal manages stress differently. I managed my stress by realizing that God was with me and in control; this knowledge gave me strength each day that I walked into the principal's office. I knew I was not alone. And I lived one day at a time. I planned ahead but I lived in the moment and made sure I had all the bases covered in areas of supervision and security. Delegating some of the responsibility to trusted employees helps tremendously with stress management.

I also managed the stress that accompanied my responsibility by living with a thankful attitude. I recall standing in the doorway to my office as I was leaving for the day while thinking how fortunate I was to be serving in this honorable position. Often, I was the last to leave in the afternoon. After securing the office, I remember standing in the doorway looking at my desk and the chair that was situated behind it. I frequently said a prayer of thanksgiving prior to closing the door. My prayer of thanksgiving would be similar to this prayer: "Thank you, God, for giving me the opportunity to serve as principal of this great school. Thank you, God, for entrusting these students to my care. Help me, Father, in all my decisions and actions to lead others in the way that you desire. I am thankful for the opportunity to serve."

Here are a few practical tips I found to be helpful for managing the stress of the principal's office:

1. Put a phone on the table beside your side of the bed along with a notepad and pencil. If you are awakened in the middle of the night with an emergency call, you will not have to search for a pencil and paper. Also, when you have a great idea in the middle of the night, you can write it on the paper and recall it the next day.

2. Keep a typed directory of your faculty and staff phone numbers along with a list of emergency contact numbers nearby. You only need to experience one emergency situation to understand how important it is to have your list of contacts readily available. Some of these contacts include the superintendent, safety director, other principals, TV stations, and so on. In stressful times, you do not want to spend fifteen minutes looking for phone numbers. Keep multiple copies of this list in secure places. For example, I kept this list of numbers in my vehicle's glove compartment, inside my kitchen cabinet, and in my briefcase, as well as in my desk at work. You cannot depend on the Internet if there is a power outage, so keep a printed copy of these important numbers at your fingertips.

3. File a directory of student names and numbers at home. You probably can access this information through the Internet if your school has a secure website for access by teachers and principals only. Still, it is helpful to have a printed copy of student numbers at home. I frequently used my student directory when I served as principal. Having one at home saved me from having to go to the office during nonwork hours when I needed to obtain a phone number.

4. Do not talk to others about confidential information. Only discuss matters with your supervisor or mentor.

5. Do not check your work email while you are at home.
6. Each day, strive to have an authentic conversation with one person with whom you work. It is easy to fall into the trap of walking through the halls saying "Good Morning. How are you?" to the people with whom you encounter without ever having a meaningful conversation. If you will slow down and focus on one authentic conversation each day, over a period of time, you will come to know the people you supervise on a deeper level.
7. Live each day with a thankful heart. I am confident that there were a number of candidates who applied for your job—and yet, you were selected for the honor of serving as the school's principal. Be thankful for the opportunity. Thank the superintendent and board of education for giving you the opportunity to serve in this honorable capacity. Remind yourself during stressful moments that you are fortunate to serve in the principal's office.
8. Remember the people who mentored you and helped you to succeed. Write them notes of appreciation from time to time. Thank them for being a positive influence in your life. Look for ways to honor these people.

Hem your blessings with thankfulness so they don't unravel.

—Author unknown

27

DO YOUR HOMEWORK

But far more important than the question of the occupation of our citizens is the question of how their family life is conducted. No matter what that occupation may be, as long as there is a real home and as long as those who make up that home do their duty to one another, to their neighbors and to the State, it is of minor consequence whether the man's trade is plied in the country or in the city, whether it calls for the work of the hands or for the work of the head.

—Theodore Roosevelt

When I began my graduate work while working full-time as a high school assistant principal, Coach Ronnie Stapler told me he was proud of me for pursuing this advanced degree. However, he cautioned me to remember to do my *home*work. He went on to explain that I needed to take care of my husband Wholey during the process of obtaining my doctorate. Occasionally, when Coach Stapler and I passed each other in the hall, he would smile and ask me if I was taking care of my *home*work. His wise advice stays with me even today, almost twenty years later.

While you are in the principal's office, do not become consumed with its demands and meanwhile neglect your family. Always make your family your number-one priority. Take care of them. Do not put them last on your list of "things to do."

When I was a high school principal, I remember leaving school late one afternoon to meet my husband for supper at a local restaurant. When I arrived fifteen minutes late, I found him sitting on a bench outside of the restaurant waiting on me. I remember feeling sad about making him wait on me. You see, someone had approached me as I was leaving the school and that was the reason I was late. It was always a challenge for me to be on time to meetings, in general, because it seemed many people needed "just a minute" of my time. That night, I determined that I would not make my husband wait on me again. I decided to put him first.

Now, if someone approaches me as I am leaving to go to a meeting or to meet Wholey, I tell the person to walk and talk with me as I go to my car. I explain that I must leave now but will be happy to meet with the person at a later date. I also learned to leave an extra fifteen minutes before I need to leave in order to be on time. Arriving a few minutes early is relaxing. I learned to appreciate having a few minutes before a meeting begins to get a cup of coffee or visit the restroom. I also enjoy not feeling rushed and having an opportunity to visit with my colleagues before the meeting starts. I have to continually work on my time management and it remains a struggle for me.

Cherish the relationships in your life. Put family and friends first after work hours. Remember to do your *home*work. Make your loved ones feel as special as they truly are to you. Spend time together; be on time when you meet. Don't forget to save some of your energy for home.

Enjoy each treasured moment with your loved ones. By doing so, you are doing your *home*work and prioritizing what is most important in your life.

Do your home*work*.

—Coach Ronnie Stapler

LET WORK BE WORK AND HOME BE HOME

We live a world where people are confused about where work is located and where home is located. A number of my colleagues respond to emails at 10:34 p.m. I see their cars in the school parking lots in the evenings and on weekends. I have overheard colleagues sigh and explain that they are glad to get back to work on Monday to get some rest whereas years ago, people went home to rest at night and on the weekends. What happened?

We are confused. Some people seem to work 24 hours a day, 7 days a week. One of my colleagues lamented that his son, a high school principal, works all the time. He told me that his son was not married and that he never made time to seek a relationship with anyone. Besides, he quipped, who would put up with the hours he keeps?

Don't make the mistake of believing the myth that the school will crumble if you are not there. Believe me; your school will continue to be functional long after you are gone. I remember when I first became principal, I worked entirely too many hours. My father asked me why I could not get my work done during the hours the board of education paid me to work. This question made me realize I needed to examine the way I spent my time at work. I still strive to follow his encouragement to get my work done during the workday.

The principal's job is unending and the work can consume your life if you let it. I continue to struggle with overworking now as a superintendent. This is the most difficult area for me to control as an administrator.

Because of increased, more efficient technology, we are tempted to work incessantly. Previously, we could go on vacation and truly be on vacation. But because of portable email devices, cell phones, and laptops, we hardly ever are 100 percent away from work. It is a challenge to truly be away from the office in today's high-tech society. One of my current board members who used to be the president of the school board encouraged me to quit sending out email on the weekends and to just enjoy my weekends. This was good advice and, while I don't always hold to it, I often think about it and it often keeps me from becoming consumed with trying to stay caught up on email on the weekends. As a principal in today's world, don't forget that email can be a serious distraction to your work productivity because you can check it anywhere and at any time of the day or night.

Let your work be work. Give a day's work for a day's pay. But when you enter the doorway of your sanctuary at home, turn off your computer, take off your shoes, and enjoy being at home. When a person approaches the end of life, I do not believe anyone wishes he or she had spent more hours at work. I believe this can be a time of regret if too much time was given to work instead of family.

Cook out with your family. Play, read, and watch movies together. Go for walks, take vacations, relax, talk, and listen. Unwind; take care of your business at home so that your life is orderly and less stressful. Let your work at home be chores at home—not work you brought home from the office. Sure, there will be times when it is necessary to finish work at home in the evening or on the weekend but this should be the exception and not the rule.

Let work be work. Let home be home. Each day is a treasured gift to be cherished and honored.

Yesterday is history. Tomorrow is a mystery. Today is a gift.

—Eleanor Roosevelt

SUMMARY OF PART IV
KEYS FOR EMOTIONAL BALANCE

1. Maintain Teflon mentality. Be strong mentally like a walnut—not thin-skinned like a grape.
2. Do not let the turkeys get you down. Realize that there will always be naysayers in every organization. This is part of life. Focus on the positive at your school and do not let the small percentage of complainers make you feel defeated.
3. Delegate your work. Enlist the help of those you supervise to do the work of the school. Focus on the large tasks that you were hired to do. Do not miss the big calling because you were focusing on small matters that did not need your attention.
4. Create inspiring and productive learning environments for you and your staff and students. Remove clutter in your office and throughout the school. Have exceptional lighting and clean tables on which to work. Maintain a safe and clean facility at all times. Have a comfortable chair behind your desk.
5. Forgive others. Begin each day with a clean slate by erasing mistakes. Do not hold grudges and do not focus on the negative actions of others. Remember that their actions reveal more about them than they do about the person or organization they are criticizing.
6. Manage stress by living one day at a time. Be organized and have information readily available in the event of an emergency.
7. Do not check work email at home.
8. Live with a thankful attitude. Thank those who gave you the opportunity to serve as principal and communicate your thankfulness to those you supervise.

9. Be confidential in all matters that occur at the school.
10. Be loyal to the system for which you work. Do not criticize its leadership publicly.
11. Do your *home*work. Make home matters a high priority.

CONCLUSION

Life in the principal's office is not easy. It is not for the weak. The leader who will inhabit the principal's office must possess physical stamina, intellectual strength, emotional resilience, and spiritual depth. The effective principal will strive for balance in each of these four areas. In spite of these lofty requirements, it is most gratifying to serve in this honorable position because you have the opportunity to help children. It is humbling to recognize the fact that your decisions, as principal, will affect the future of your school and its students and staff. This truth is a serious responsibility.

When I served as principal, I never worked harder in my life. But, because my work was in concert with my skills and abilities—and with my mission in life—it was extremely satisfying. I knew what my job was and I vigorously assumed my duties. In addition to my regular duties, I wanted to go the extra mile. I wanted to do my normal work on a daily basis and then look for one more priority to add to my list of things to do.

When I was a young girl, I vividly remember one afternoon when my mother was getting ready for Daddy to come home from work. I remember her taking a bath and putting on fresh clothes and make-up. I asked her why she was doing this. After all, it was only Daddy coming home, I said. Mother told me that Daddy did not deserve to come home to a maid. He works hard each day and is surrounded by other ladies who are well groomed, she said. She explained that she wanted to also be well groomed and attractive for him when he came home at night.

Mother told me that each person in our family has a job. She explained that Daddy's job was to earn the living for us to have a home, clothes, and food. Mother said it was her job to take care of my dad, my sister, and me. She was responsible for our home, our food, and us. She said she did this job during the hours Daddy worked and while we were in school so that we could all be together and relax when we were at home. Other than cooking, my mother never did housework such as cleaning or laundry at night or on the weekends; she did this work and ran errands during the day while we were at work and school. Mother explained to me that my job was to go to school and make good grades. She reiterated the fact that everybody in our family has a job.

With this story in mind, I ask you to consider for yourself, as principal, "What is my job?" It is important to be able to answer this question. If you can answer this question, you will be able to focus and prioritize each day's work to your satisfaction. Your answer will guide you during your journey. The job of being a principal is definitely multifaceted. Your attention will oscillate between issues throughout the day. However, the tasks are all achievable if you properly plan, stay organized, and truly know your role and responsibilities. What was my job when I served as principal? My job was to provide a safe and healthy environment for my students so that productive and meaningful learning could occur with competent, effective teachers. Remember, we do not have schools so that people will have jobs. We have schools so that students will learn and become productive citizens one day.

Yes, it is difficult, but rewarding to serve as principal. Schools are characterized by myriad activities and events each day. As principal, you will often feel like getting your work completed each day is like putting a size 8 *foot* into a size 7 *shoe*! You will have a plethora of issues aimed at you from the minute you enter the door until you leave at the end of the day. The principal's job is hard but is also satisfying if it is your calling to serve. The good days will definitely outweigh the challenging days.

Live one day at a time. Enjoy the journey while you are in the principal's office because you will not repeat the experience. Each year and each day will be unique and special. Consider a couple of "what ifs?" each morning as you start your day:

What if this morning was the last time I saw my family?
What if today is the last day I interact with my faculty, staff, and students?

How would your attitude change? What would you do differently if the "what if" became a reality? Consider these two "what ifs" each day: It may lead you to making sure you take the appropriate time with your family each and every morning to show them how much they mean to you before rushing out the door to work, and it may make you a little more compassionate in your dealings with faculty, staff, and students. I close with a few final words of advice for you, my friend, as you begin or continue your journey in the principal's office:

1. Strive to maintain balance in the physical, intellectual, emotional, and spiritual (PIES) areas of your life.
2. Seek wisdom. Reading a chapter of King Solomon's Proverbs each day is a good place to start. Also, enlist the help of a mentor.

3. Keep a holistic vision for your school and plan for the future.
4. Do not be wasteful. Do not waste time, money, or materials entrusted to you.
5. Move slowly and with deliberation in all actions.
6. Employ a bank teller's mentality: Finish one task before beginning another.
7. Live in the present and plan for the future. Learn from your mistakes but do not dwell on them. Don't look back. Remember the story of Lot's wife in chapter 19 of Genesis. The angels told Lot, his wife and daughters to flee the city and to not look back. However, Lot's wife looked back and she became a pillar of salt. If you visit the Dead Sea, you will see salt formations that remind us of her disobedience. Do not look back.
8. Forgive and forget others' mistakes and your own. Don't be so hard on yourself.
9. Love and protect the children that God is entrusting to your care.
10. Remember you will only pass this way once. Enjoy the journey!

In closing, I hope you will enjoy serving as principal as much as I did. Some of the happiest memories of my life are contained in my mental scrapbook of days I served in the principal's office. It was there that I learned some of the greatest lessons about life.

I am not an expert on any matter discussed in this book. I do not claim to have all of the answers. I am a practitioner, not a scholar. I am one who has learned lessons during my journey through my successes, my mistakes, and from watching others. I am simply one who is willing to share these lessons.

It is my sincere hope that this primer will assist you in your journey. May God bless you because of your willingness to serve as principal in order to help others. Through your efforts, our world will be a better place to live for future generations.

From everyone who has been given much, much will be demanded . . .

—Jesus in Luke 12:48 (NIV)

100 RULES FOR
BALANCED LEADERSHIP

INTRODUCTION

1. In order to be a successful principal, it is essential to look inward and obtain an understanding of self before attempting to lead others.
2. In understanding one's self, it is helpful to examine the four areas of our being. These areas are the physical, intellectual, emotional, and spiritual parts of our existence. Some people refer to these areas by the acronym PIES. Work to maintain balance in these four areas.
3. Each action in life can be placed into one of these four domains; there are some areas that overlap between domains. A few examples of activities that are classified in each area follow.
4. In the physical domain, we can find activities such as diet, exercise, sleep, grooming, posture, manners, and communication.
5. In the intellectual domain, we can find activities such as education, work, study, knowledge, organizing, analyzing, and writing.
6. In the emotional domain, we can find activities such as relationships, social events, self-esteem, stress, creativity, worry, and forgiveness.
7. In the spiritual domain, we can find activities such as mission, beliefs, values, worship, prayer, service, and study.
8. Once we understand and recognize these areas in our lives, we are then able to master strengths in each area thereby creating a mentally, physically, emotionally, and spiritually stronger being.

SPIRITUAL BALANCE

9. Define your mission, foundation, values, and beliefs. Together, these important parts of your spiritual being form your internal glue. They strengthen you and keep you together in times of stress and examinations.

10. Renew and refine each day. You will strengthen your internal glue by seeking continual growth and improvement in all areas of your life.

11. What are your favorite things in life that simply make you happy? Define your favorite things and write them in your journal. Then, schedule time to enjoy your favorite things in order to renew your spirit.

12. Separate your personal values and beliefs from the values and principles that govern our country. Understand and separate "church and state." Do not let your beliefs influence your decisions when you know your belief is in direct opposition to the law.

13. Live a proactive life in the principal's office. Avoid mistakes or "potholes" by first identifying them. Then, avoid potholes through accountability. Seek further accountability through guidance from a trusted mentor.

14. Be vigilant when handling school money. Always have two people present when counting money. Deposit cash at the bank daily. Supervise those individuals charged with the responsibility for handling money watchfully.

15. Model your beliefs daily. The principal serves as a model for character education both in and out of the principal's office.

16. Be honest.

17. Remember the Golden Rule: Treat other people the way you want to be treated.

18. When you talk about other people, pretend the person is seated in the room. Do not make a statement that you would not make to the person directly.

19. Help others by encouraging them and guiding them through difficult situations.

20. Encourage others by giving them credit when credit is due.

21. Defuse situations by "putting a little light on them." Instead of whispering about newsflashes, employees will know the true story and return to the focus of the school—teaching and learning.

22. Manage stress in an effective manner twenty-four hours a day, seven days a week. Understand that you are the fish in the fishbowl. People are watching you. Acknowledging this truth will strengthen you as you "direct traffic naked."

23. Be you! Proudly stand as an original.

24. Trust your instincts in all you do. You are a respected individual. You have been given the keys to your building and responsibility for the total program

at your school. Boldly display your personality through your attitude and actions on a daily basis.

PHYSICAL BALANCE

25. Take care of your body. Just as you must maintain your vehicle, it is imperative that you take care of your body though rest, play, and exercise, as well as through preventive measures such as having physicals.
26. Worry and turmoil are not good bedfellows. When you consistently treat your students and employees fairly, you will not toss and turn at night worrying about the decisions you made. Display consistency while applying the rules and you will be postured to sleep like a baby at night because you have a clear conscience.
27. Make time for play at school and at home.
28. When you are observing physical education classes, get involved occasionally by throwing the ball or even wearing gym clothes one day and sharing a day in the gym with your students to show them you believe in exercise and lifelong wellness activities.
29. Fuel your body with nutritious food each day. Avoid junk food.
30. Deliver the best physical presentation you can as principal of your school. Arrive at school each day refreshed, well groomed, and attractively dressed in professional attire.
31. Wear sensible shoes to work each day.
32. Practice good posture for presentation and health benefits.
33. Display impeccable manners that will put others at ease.
34. Know how to properly shake hands and make introductions.
35. Utilize effective communication techniques. Listen more than you talk when meeting with others.
36. Smile and display positive body language.
37. Return phone calls and answer emails.
38. Walk with enthusiasm and energy.
39. Effectively use your time each day in order to maximize your task accomplishments during a day. Do not waste time by standing around talking unnecessarily. Give others the time they need when they are asking for help, then manage this time efficiently by listening, taking notes, and summarizing the details of the conference.
40. Do not rely upon your own memory. Enlist the help of a Little Black Book and use mapping techniques to help you remember others' names and descriptive information.
41. Complete tasks as soon as possible. Do not procrastinate. Procrastination drains you intellectually because you are continually thinking about the task that is yet to be done.

INTELLECTUAL BALANCE

42. Be professional at all times.
43. Understand the scope of your responsibility as principal and the organizational chart of your school system.
44. Know the chain of command and follow it to communicate and conduct business.
45. Stick to the book. Use board policy to ground every decision you make as principal. Be knowledgeable about state and federal laws that affect school administration.
46. Become proficient at conducting conferences. Allow ample time to listen to others' concerns.
47. Create a student handbook and communicate its contents to all of your students and parents. Have students and parents sign a document acknowledging receipt of this important handbook that provides an operational foundation for your school.
48. Create plans for every imaginable situation. Some of these plans are mandated by your state department of education, while others will be plans you create to promote an awareness of possible situations that could occur during your tenure as principal.
49. Build your winning team by carefully selecting each team member. Thoroughly review resumes and application packets. Take time to have an in-depth interview with each potential candidate and do not forget to check references.
50. Mentor new teachers and staff by assigning an official mentor to them. Also, mentor these employees yourself through conversations, meetings, and observations.
51. Improve employees' performance through accountability and communication of high expectations.
52. Create a shared vision for your school's success with the input of all stakeholders.
53. Build morale in your school by establishing relationships and initiating times of fellowship. Enthusiastically promote school-spirit items such as t-shirts.
54. Remember the written word is the most powerful form of communication because it is everlasting.
55. Be careful about what you put in writing! Is it accurate? Is it grammatically correct?
56. Visualize your newly created written document on the front page of your newspaper; it could be printed there one day. Be proud of each document you create.
57. Be fair, firm, and consistent in matters of discipline and employee supervision.
58. Treat all people with whom you interact with kindness and respect.
59. Model effective use of twenty-first-century technology.

60. Be a lifelong learner.
61. Tell your school's story to all stakeholders through public speaking opportunities, websites, and annual reports.
62. Speak about your school to others with enthusiasm and confidence.
63. Avoid politics. Do not publicly support candidates for election.
64. Do communicate your students' needs to elected officials within the perimeter of the legislative process. Support education in your system, state, and nation.
65. Read, study, and turn off the television!

EMOTIONAL BALANCE

66. Maintain Teflon mentality.
67. Be strong mentally like a walnut—not thin-skinned like a grape.
68. Do not let the turkeys get you down. Realize that there will be naysayers in every organization. This is part of life. Focus on the positive at your school and do not let the small percentage of complainers make you feel defeated.
69. Delegate. Enlist the help of those you supervise to do the work of the school. Focus on the large tasks that you were hired to do. Do not miss the big picture because you were focusing on small matters that did not demand your attention.
70. Create inspiring and productive learning environments for you and your staff and students.
71. Clean your desk regularly.
72. Have a student-created artifact such as a drawing or piece of pottery on your desk to remind you why you are in the principal's office.
73. Maintain a safe and clean facility at all times.
74. Remove clutter in your office and throughout the school.
75. Have exceptional lighting throughout the school.
76. Place a lamp on your desk to provide additional lighting while working.
77. Have a comfortable chair behind your desk.
78. Consider having an alternate surface to work upon while enabling you to stand such as a counter or podium.
79. Take care of your faculty and staff and provide them with the tools they need in order to be successful.
80. Forgive. Begin each day with a clean slate. Erase the mistakes that were directed at you or your school from your memory. Look for ways to help others.
81. Do not hold grudges and do not focus on the negative actions of others. Wisely note that their actions reveal more about them than they do about the person or organization they are criticizing.
82. Manage stress by living one day at a time.
83. Be organized and have information readily available in the event of an emergency.

84. Do not check work email at home.
85. Strive to have an authentic conversation with one person with whom you work each day.
86. Live with a thankful attitude. Thank those who gave you the opportunity to serve as principal and communicate your thankfulness to serve to those you supervise.
87. Be confidential in all matters that occur at the school.
88. Be loyal to the system for which you work. Do not criticize its leadership publicly.
89. Do your homework. Make home matters a high priority.

FINAL WORDS OF ADVICE

90. Move slowly and with deliberation in all actions.
91. Employ a bank teller's mentality: Finish one task before beginning another.
92. Do not be wasteful. Do not waste time, talents, money, or materials entrusted to you. Be a good steward of all the gifts you have been given.
93. Seek wisdom. Read one chapter of King Solomon's Proverbs in the Holy Bible each day. There are 31 chapters; read the chapter that corresponds to the day of the month.
94. Work to maintain PIES balance and continual improvement in the spiritual, physical, intellectual, and emotional areas of your life.
95. Don't look back at your past mistakes. Remember the story of Lot's wife in chapter 19 of Genesis. The angels told Lot, his wife and daughters to flee from the city and to not look back. However, Lot's wife looked back and she became a pillar of salt. If you visit the Dead Sea, you will see salt formations that remind us to not look back and dwell on the past.
96. Treat yourself in the same manner that you would treat an employee or student.
97. Keep a holistic vision for your school and plan for the future.
98. Love and protect the children that God is entrusting to your care.
99. Mentor others along the way.
100. Remember you will only pass this way once. We are only here for a little while, so enjoy the journey.

B

LETTER OF COMMENDATION

Huntsville High School

2304 Billie Watkins Drive
Huntsville, Alabama 35801

Jan Harris, Ed.D.
Principal

Telephone
(256) 428-8050

December 9, 2002

Coach Melanie Donahoo
Teacher, Volleyball and Basketball Coach
Huntsville High School

Dear Coach Donahoo,

Congratulations to you and your team for winning the 2002 Alabama State Volleyball Championship! This is an accomplishment that you will remember and treasure the rest of your life. I will always fondly recall the memories at the State Playoffs. What an exciting display of energy, enthusiasm, teamwork, and talent on the part of our truly exceptional girls! Additionally, it is a pleasure for me to commend you all for setting a new Alabama State record for volleyball wins!

You are a tremendous coach, teacher and role model for our students at Huntsville High School. Hiring you was one of the easiest and best decisions I have made during my administrative career. Your high standards inspire and motivate others to strive for greatness. With your leadership, your volleyball players are leaders on and off the court. They are to be admired because of their dedication to your shared vision of winning the State championship.

Thank you for your dedication to the youth of our community. It is with great Panther pride that I congratulate you on a job well done and for being voted by your colleagues as Huntsville Coach of the Year! Go Big Red!

Sincerely yours,

Jan Harris

Jan Harris, Ed.D.
Principal

Copy: Dr. Ann Moore, Superintendent
Human Resources – Personnel File of Melanie Donahoo

C

LITTLE BLACK BOOK ENTRY

Little Black Book

Sample Entry (Names are Fictitious)

August 2003

Personnel

(Retired)

John Brown
(English)

Ellen Smith
(Math)

(Hired)

Bill Jones
(English)

Kathleen Wilson
(Math)

(Resigned)

Charles Carter
(Social Studies)
(moved to GA)

(Hired)

Nancy Wilcox
(Social Studies)

Facility

Replaced Exterior Doors on West side of Gym

Planted 2 Oak Trees at main entrance

Repaired roof over auditorium

Gifts   Senator Peter Burkett $5000 for
technology

D

MEMO

April 3, 2000

To: Faculty, Parents and Students

From: Jan Harris, Principal *Jan Harris*
      Whitesburg Middle School

Re: **SAT Testing April 7, 10, 11, 12**

On Friday, April 7, 2000, we begin SAT testing! Testing will continue on Monday the 10th through Wednesday the 12th. Testing should conclude each day no later than 11:30 a.m. Students should be present each of these days and not check out (if possible) since there is no make-up test given. On Thursday the 6th, students will take a practice SAT test during homeroom. This test will conclude at 9:30 a.m. The schedule is as follows:

Thursday, April 6th	**Practice Test ends at 9:30 a.m.**
Friday, April 7th	**OLSAT ends at 10:30 a.m.**
Monday, April 10th	**SAT Reading and Vocabulary ends at 11:30 a.m.**
Tuesday, April 11th	**SAT Math ends at 11:30 a.m.** *(students should bring calculator)*
Wednesday, April 12th	**SAT Language, Science and Social Studies ends at 11:30 a.m.**

For best results, students are encouraged to get a **good night's sleep**. Additionally, they should **eat a nutritious breakfast** before school. Students should **bring two #2 pencils and a book to read** after completion of each sub-test. **No homework** will be assigned during SAT testing Thursday through Tuesday.

Below is an analysis of our exemplary test history at WMS. The national average is 50%. As you can see, our students have done extremely well. We are accustomed to having the top test scores in the city!

YEAR	SIXTH GRADE	SEVENTH GRADE	EIXTH GRADE
1999	82%	84%	82%
1998	81%	80%	80%
1997	81%	83%	84%
1996	84%	83%	84%

Congratulations! I am so very proud of our teachers' efforts, parent participation, and student performance. I look forward to our scores this year. We usually receive the scores before school is out for the summer.

E

WEEKLY CALENDAR

Calendar for April 3 - 14
From the Principal's Office
Dr. Jan Harris

Monday the 3rd
        PTA Board Meeting @ 7 p.m. in the Library
Tuesday the 4th
        Retirement Incentive Mtg @ Butler High Auditorium @ 3:45p.m.
Wednesday the 5th
        Faculty Meeting
Thursday the 6th
        Track Meet
        HCS Board Work Session (Strategic Planning will be presented)
                5:30 p.m. @ Butler High Auditorium
Friday the 7th
        5th six weeks ends
        OLSAT
        Choral Spring Dance 6:30 p.m. – 9:30 p.m.
Monday the 10th
        6th six weeks begins
        SAT
Tuesday the 11th
        SAT
Wednesday the 12th
        SAT
        Track City Meet @ 1p.m.
Thursday the 13th
        All-State Band to Auburn
Friday the 14th
        All-State Band to Auburn

ANNUAL REPORT

DR. JAN HARRIS
PRINCIPAL

Executive Summary 2001-02

HUNTSVILLE HIGH SCHOOL

Huntsville High School
Go Big Red!

HUNTSVILLE HIGH
FOUNDED 1908

Huntsville High School
2304 Billie Watkins Ave.
Huntsville, Al 35801
Phone: 256-428-8050
Fax: 256-428-8051
Email: jharris@hsv.k12.al.us

HHS AWARDS

NASA/Marshall's Great Moon Buggy Race—1st in the state and 4th in the nation! Sponsor—Takellyne Brown Engineering, Mr. Del O'Neal & Mr. Wayne Mullins

Operation Green Team Campus Beautification Award (4th consecutive year)- Sponsor—PTSA Choir Linda Frost, Student Council & Ms. Dottie Fuller

American Scholastic Press 1st Place Award—HHS Literary Magazine Spectrum - Sponsor Karen Wilkerson

Girls Soccer State Champions Sponsor—Mrs. Pat Moore & Coach Henry Napiogi

Volleyball—3rd in the State - Coach Hutchison

Baseball Final 8 in the State- Coach Mark Mincher

PTSA Awards – Mrs. Jan Ingram, President

Alabama PTA Newspaper Award (Dolni Giery Mancey & Becky Sparks)

Alabama PTA Membership Award (Chair—Noel Saunders)

Huntsville Council of PTA's Journalism Award (Chairs Giney Mancey & Becky Sparks)

Huntsville Council of PTA's Cultural Arts Award (Chair Harriet Frederick)

Huntsville Council of PTA's Character & Spiritual Education Award (Chairs Lisa Parker & Lisa Stroud)

Faculty Awards

HHS & PTSA Teacher of the Year—Mr. Scott Sharp

HCS Aspiring Administrators Academy - Jeanie Barnes

HCS Prospective Principals Academy - Mrs. Leslie Emswiller

HCS Superintendent Preparation Academy - Dr. Jan Harris

HCS Coach of the Year

Mark Mincher—baseball

Lynne Abernathy—tennis

Jennifer Hutchison—volleyball

Huntsville High School Highlights 2001-02

Continued work on new $25 million building—ground breaking—December 2002

Four National Merit Finalists

Four National Merit Commended Scholars

One National Achievement Scholar

One National Achievement Participant

Class of 2002 earned $5,773,205 in scholarships

$46,100 spent on technology

Award winning programs in band, choral, theatre, and vocational education

Musical - The Wizard of Oz, Director Mike Choppell

Average Scores ACT— 22.5,

SAT—Verbal 577, Math 566, Total 1142

Pass Rate for AL High School Graduation Exam:

Reading 99%, Language 98%,

Science 98%, Math 97%

~~~~~

Pictured on front from left to right: Back Row - Vicki Caquias, Lauren Callaway, Debbie Jolliff, Wayne Jensen, Emily Caneer, Lynda Senkbeil, Front Row - Martha Sharp, Leslie Eaneault, Jan Harris

~~~~~

Accredited

Southern Association of Colleges and Schools

Grade Summary

Grade 9—325

Grade 10—248

Grade 11—217

Grade 12—254

Total Number of Students = 1044

Membership by Ethnicity

White—83%

Black—14%

Asian—2%

Indian, Hispanic—1%

Theme for the Year

Bricks & Shoes

Expectations

Treat other people the way you want to be treated...walk in their shoes.

We are building a new school. Each day, we build our lives... one brick at a time we lay our future's foundation.

Advanced Placement Scores

Subject, % Students who earned a 3 or higher, # taking the exam, Teacher

US History, 100%, 37, Nancy Butler

Biology, 87%, 15, Judy Kirk

Calculus AB, 97%, 34, Scott Sharp

Chemistry, 73%, 15, Ken Silvernail

Computer Science, 0%, 2, Delilah Smith

Economics, 100%, 2, Jenny Barrett

Eng. Lang/Comp, 67%, 54, Becky McDowell

Eng. Lit/Comp, 76%, 58, Julie Culpepper

Gov &Pol US, 0%, 4, Lee Farless

Physics, 23%, 13, Del O'Neal

Superintendent Ann Roy Moore with Principal Jan Harris at HHS Graduation 2002

EPILOGUE

Earline Pinckley

In her preface to this book, Jan very kindly mentioned that I was her mentor. She also mentioned my response to her expression of gratitude, when I simply said she could repay me by helping others along the way. The book she has written will fulfill that promise by offering the kind of practical, down-to-earth advice that every administrator craves. I have no doubt that the book arises out of Jan's genuine desire to be a mentor to other school administrators.

Jan came to our school as a bright, enthusiastic, young mathematics teacher, and she told me very quickly that her goal was to be an administrator. Every administrator knows that one of the most difficult tasks of a principal is finding willing staff members to assume the many extracurricular duties that are so important to the school. The jobs are time-consuming and often unremunerated. But, especially at the secondary level, they are critical to the success of the school. We administrators were constantly seeking staff members who were capable and willing to fill these rolls. On my advice, Jan volunteered to sponsor the junior class. That job included a huge commitment of time and energy, because the junior class sponsor was responsible for the *prom*. Most people have little concept of the time that teachers like Jan are willing to give, but the school principal holds enormous appreciation for those teachers, and the principal often recognizes an aptitude for administration in the performance of such tasks.

Jan's handling of the prom led all of us to see her potential as an administrator, and I encouraged her to enroll in an Ed.D. program to prepare to be a principal. When she selected her committee, she asked me to serve, and I was given the opportunity to observe her development from teacher to administrator. Ironically, when the principal who gave Jan her first promotion to administration was trying to come to a decision, he asked for my advice. He was considering Jan—who at the time was only twenty-eight years of age—and an older, very intelligent staff member. I remember his comments as he was mulling over his decision, his concern about Jan's youth, and his feelings of obligation to the longer tenure of the other person. His final decision came down to Jan's sponsorship of the junior class. She had worked to earn the position, well beyond the effort required to complete an Ed.D. In doing so, she had demonstrated an understanding of the total effort required to keep a school running effectively. The other person had an equal education, high intelligence, and love of students and faculty but lacked the total picture. Hence, Jan's discussion of balance reflects the kind of understanding that any effective administrator must have.

Jan is generous in attributing mentorship to me but Jan actually needed no mentor. She has the drive and focus to accomplish her goals independently. However, I did participate in her advancement, and I appreciate her recognition of my contributions. In fact, every effective teacher is a mentor. Being a mentor requires a person to set self aside and focus on the needs of another person, whether a student or staff member, as well as the needs of the organization. Therefore, I can, with all humility, take great pride in Jan's achievements.

I especially appreciated Jan's inclusion of spiritual balance as a necessary component of the effective administrator, because it is through the great spiritual leaders that we are able to see examples of mentorship in the ideal. Christians are taught that Jesus was balanced, just as Jan's vision is balanced, "in wisdom, and in stature, and in favor with God and men" (Luke 2:52). He was the supreme mentor. I have also served as a formal mentor for newly appointed administrators, but I believe that the most effective mentors are those who seek to help another person out of a genuine desire to help that person achieve his or her personal goals. I really believe that most people are kind, and will respond with help if a person, like Jan, simply asks.

The title of Epilogue for my comments carries a connotation of finality that seems inappropriate with this author. Jan is still young and still has much to offer the educational world. I believe that I should just call this To Be Continued . . .

With Love,
Earline Pinckley

REFERENCES

Buckner, S., and J. Gonzalez (March 30, 2005). Americans spend more than 100 hours commuting to work each year, Census Bureau reports: New York and Maryland residents face most time traveling to work. *U.S. Bureau Census Bureau News* (CB05-AC.02). Washington, DC: U.S. Department of Commerce. Retrieved February 7, 2008, from http://www.census.gov/Press-Release/www/releases/archives/american_community_survey_acs/004489.html.

Campbell, J. (1990). *The Hero's Journey*. San Francisco: Harper & Row, specifically p. 214.

Van Biema, D. (April 2, 2007). The case for teaching the Bible. *Time* magazine, pp. 40–46.

ABOUT THE AUTHOR

Dr. Jan Irons Harris, superintendent of Cullman City Schools, received her bachelor's and master's degrees in math/education from the University of North Alabama and the University of South Carolina, respectively. She earned her doctorate in school administration from Peabody College of Vanderbilt University where she received the Wheeler Prize for Outstanding Academic Achievement.

She taught mathematics and served as a middle and high school principal before becoming superintendent. In 2001, she was named Alabama PTA High School Principal of the Year and UNA Alumnus of the Year. She is a past president of Kappa Chapter of Delta Kappa Gamma.

In Cullman, she is active in her church and community. She serves as an adult teacher and is a facilitator, along with her husband Wholey, for the Dave Ramsey Financial Peace University. Additionally, she serves on the board of directors for the Cullman Chamber of Commerce and the Cullman County United Way and is the president of the Waterford Place Homeowner's Association.

Dr. Harris has presented numerous workshops at the national and state level. She and members of the Cullman City School district have presented workshops for its successful 1:1 Laptop Initiative at Cullman Middle School. Additional statewide recognition was given for the innovative "What did you read last night?" reading campaign. She formed an Aspiring Administrators Academy in Cullman. This is her first book.

Made in the USA
Lexington, KY
19 August 2015